Words of Praise for

The Truth About Tennis

The Definitive Guide for the Recreational Player

In his new book, *The Truth About Tennis,* Greg Moran, the best coach of recreational players in the country, breaks down this complex game and provides an array of simple tips and solutions for the club player. There are "aha" moments on every page where readers will be saying, "Hey, I can do that," or "I have never considered that. Let me give it a try."

This is the ideal book for any recreational player looking for ways to improve and become a more confident and complete player. Read *The Truth About Tennis* before your opponent has the opportunity to read Greg's brilliant book.

Kirk Anderson
USTA Director of Coaching Education

Greg Moran has done it again with his latest book, *The Truth About Tennis.* Whether you're new to the game or trying to improve your rating, this book is certain to help. I especially love the section about strategy. At a time when most Rec players are addicted to perfecting their technique, the strategy section is a gold mine for people that really want to know what it takes to improve their tennis game. Do yourself a favor and get this book if you really want to learn how to play as well in matches as you do in practice.

Jorge Capestany
USPTA & PTR Master Professional, 2-time National Pro of the Year

---

With all of the analytics today, players and coaches frequently confuse the basics of playing and coaching the game. In *The Truth About Tennis,* Greg gives you the keys to unlocking the basics that have been the core since tennis began. Greg's book gives you the material to develop a mature, tactical approach to becoming the best you can be. The book is in your hand, the information is solid – now see how good you can be!

Ken DeHart
PTR Hall of Fame
PTR International Master Professional
USPTA Master Professional
USA High Performance Coach

The Truth About Tennis leaves no stone unturned, exposing many myths about tennis ultimately revealing that the truth lies in simplicity and effort over time. Greg Moran has done a wonderful job in helping recreational players maximize their potential by learning how to "park their ego" and embrace the battle of competition. If you are interested in developing your technique, strategy, improvement process, and your mindset, then this book is a must-read. It is layered with practical strategies that you can immediately apply to your game and your life.

Emma Doyle
TA High-Performance Coach, Author: *What Makes a Great Coach?*

Reading *The Truth About Tennis* provides a most enjoyable journey. Greg Moran, one of the nation's most respected and experienced teaching pros, is at his best as he addresses his passion—the recreational level player. One quickly embraces his simple and effective writing style, as well as his teaching philosophy.

Greg nails it with this great read! Congrats on a job well done!

Dick Gould
Emeritus: Men's Tennis Coach

Director of Tennis Stanford University

I can say, without reservation, that Greg Moran understands the game of tennis with great insight and intelligence. *The Truth About Tennis* provides advice that will be immensely helpful to players of any level.

Allen Fox
Ph.D.
Wimbledon Quarterfinalist
Coached Pepperdine to top 10 ranking for 10 years
Author of *Think to Win*

Yes. Yes. Yes. Finally a book that tells you the truth about tennis! Everything you need to know about our wonderful sport is detailed so expertly and with such passion that I found myself in awe at the obvious love that Greg has for teaching. All tennis players at all levels should have this book in their library.

John Loyd
Former British #1,
Wimbledon Mixed-Doubles Champion

Praise for Greg Moran's Previous Books

"A must for every tennis player's library."

Chris Evert
Tennis Legend

"Greg's advice will guarantee you more wins."

Tracy Austin
Tennis Legend

"Greg's book could be a blueprint for how I've approached the game from my junior days in Sweden through my career on the professional and senior tours."

Mats Wilander
Tennis Legend

"Club players everywhere can win more and have more fun with Greg's unique, back to the future approach to tennis."

Luke Jensen
French Open Doubles Champion

"Greg has worked with top players, studied players of all levels, participated in research and taught thousands of students. He brings an enthusiasm and passion to his teaching and writing so his book will have to be at the top of the list for all tennis lovers."

Vic Braden
Legendary Tennis Teacher

Greg Moran is one of America's most renowned and experienced tennis teaching professionals. For over forty-five years, Greg has helped players of all ages and abilities improve their tennis, win more matches, and have a great time doing it. A member of the Wilson Advisory Staff, the Cardio Tennis National Speaker's Team, and the USTA's Coach Developer program, Greg has traveled the country and to Africa conducting workshops for players and coaches.

In addition to his on-court activities, Greg is an award-winning writer. He's a frequent contributor to Tennis Magazine and is the author of the bestselling Tennis Beyond Big Shots books. Greg is the owner and Director of Tennis at the Four Seasons Racquet Club in Wilton, Conn.

To Kelley – the love of my life and the soul of our family.

Michael, Katie, Claire, and Mike – we love you and are so proud of the people you are and the lives you've built.

Olly, Molly, and Evie—find your passion and go after it every day of your lives.

Love, "Mimi" and "Pop".

Greg Moran

THE TRUTH ABOUT TENNIS

The Definitive Guide for the Recreational Player

AUSTIN MACAULEY PUBLISHERS™

LONDON * CAMBRIDGE * NEW YORK * SHARJAH

Ordering Information
Quantity sales: Special discounts are available on quantity purchases by corporations, associations, and others. For details, contact the publisher at the address below.

Publisher's Cataloging-in-Publication data
Moran, Greg
The Truth About Tennis

ISBN 9798886934632 (Paperback)
ISBN 9798886934649 (ePub e-book)

Library of Congress Control Number: 2023918052

www.austinmacauley.com/us

First Published 2024
Austin Macauley Publishers LLC
40 Wall Street, 33rd Floor, Suite 3302
New York, NY 10005
USA

mail-usa@austinmacauley.com
+1 (646) 5125767

The journey that resulted in this book has truly been a team effort. I'd like to express my gratitude to the members of my team for helping to make *The Truth About Tennis* a reality.

Paul Fein, Kent Oswald, Jay Fielden and James Martin who provided me with invaluable expertise and guidance during the writing and editing process.

All the tennis teachers (past and present) who ignited and fueled my passion for the game and whose wisdom shaped the way I approach teaching, writing, and playing tennis.

Finally, to the team at Austin Macauley Publishing.

To you all, I say a very sincere and a heartfelt thank you.

– Greg Moran

Table of Contents

Note to the Reader

The explanations and instructions in this book are given from a right-handed player's perspective. Left-handed players should reverse the references from right to left.

For ease of reading, the text uses the terms 'he' and 'his' but those terms are meant to include "she" and "hers".

Foreword by Rick Macci

Whether it's coaching all-time greats such as the Williams sisters, Andy Roddick, Jennifer Capriati, and Maria Sharapova, or working with a 4-year-old beginner, I've always said that my favorite student is the one who's across the net from me.

After over 40 years, teaching tennis is still my passion. I wake up every day at 3:30 a.m. and give lessons, seven days a week, to anyone at any age. Greg Moran is cut from the same mold.

Though he's a late riser (5:00 a.m. LOL), Greg is also on the court Monday-Sunday teaching tennis. His passion lies with the recreational player. He introduces beginners to the game, teaches the working warriors and stay-at-home moms. He trains USTA teams, highly ranked players and high school students whose dream is to make their varsity team. Greg knows the goals of the recreational player and he wrote *The Truth About Tennis* to help them achieve them.

Forty years into his career, Greg remains a true student of the game. Eager to learn new drills, techniques or other ways to connect with his students, Greg studies the great tennis teachers of the past and picks the brains of the top coaches today. That's how I first met Greg—a 5:00 am email with some questions about working with juniors.

Greg's approach to teaching tennis is straightforward and so is his book. In Part 1, you'll learn three important truths that will set you on the path to becoming a better player.

In Parts 2–4, Greg will go over the key (often overlooked) elements of strokes, strategy, and the mental game. In Part 5, you'll learn how to design your personal program for improvement. At the end of the book, Greg has included a bonus section on doubles.

As you read Greg's book, you'll feel as if you're out on the court with him. His writing style is casual, and his information is spot on. If you're a serious recreational player looking to improve your game, *The Truth About Tennis* is a must read.

Rick Macci

Personal coach for five world #1 players
8 Grand Slam champions
322 National Titles
7-time Coach of the Year
Youngest ever inducted into the USPTA Hall of Fame
Featured in the Academy Award-winning film, *King Richard*

Introduction
The Truth Is...

Tennis instruction today has become far too complicated, there's too much of it, and a lot of it is just not good for you.

If you type the words 'tennis instruction' into your internet search engine, you'll see more than 50 million results. Amazon can sell you more than 10,000 products to improve your game, and there are an endless number of apps and podcasts that promise to make you a high-level player simply by unlocking your phone.

Each of these instructional opportunities teases you with the "secret" to success or a "revolutionary" approach to the game. Many involve playing like the pros—perhaps the single most ridiculous piece of advice a recreational tennis player can be given. I'll explain why as we move along.

Combined with this information overload is the fact that people's approach to learning has changed. Years ago, a player would study under one instructor. They had their tennis guru who had his approach to teaching the game. The student stayed with that teacher for an extended period of time. They developed a rapport, and the learning experience was an enjoyable and successful adventure. The player improved and had fun doing it.

Today, many players take lessons from several different instructors, some of whom have absolutely no business teaching tennis. Steve Smith, founder of Greatbasetennis.com, a website dedicated to improving the quality of tennis teaching, calls them "car trunk pros." All they have is "a ball hopper and an ego," says Steve.

Then there's this fun fact: a recent study from Microsoft determined that the average person today has an attention span of only eight seconds, down from 12 seconds in the year 2000. Disturbing to say the least, however, it is what it is.

Today's attention-challenged player is bombarded with massive amounts of complex, contradicting, and sometimes incorrect information. They're then expected to absorb and apply that data to reach their tennis potential. Quite honestly, they haven't got a chance, which is why I had to write this book.

I've been playing, teaching, reading, and writing about tennis for more than 50 years. Far more important, I've spent over 100,000 hours on the court with players just like you. If I've learned one thing, it's that success on the tennis court at every level can be found in one word—simplicity.

Vic Braden, who I believe was the greatest tennis teacher of all time, once said to me that "the better a player becomes, the simpler his approach to the game must be." As my experience working with recreational players of all levels has grown, Vic's words have become prophetic. Today's players improve the fastest when instruction is delivered quickly, simply, and honestly.

When I teach, I'll often ask my players if they want the country club lesson or the USTA lesson. When asked the difference, I explain that, with the country club lesson, I tell them how wonderful they are. With the USTA lesson, I tell it like it is. This book will tell it to you like it is.

I'm going to help you cut down on the inner chatter and information overload and give your path to improvement a reset. I want to refocus your attention on the key elements of the game to take your tennis to the next level.

This book contains no "secrets" and will not offer a "revolutionary" approach. There are no such things, and if someone tells you they have them, hide your credit card. Instead, the following pages will offer tennis wisdom and, as Scottish author and politician Hugh Kerr once famously said:

All wisdom is plagiarism; only stupidity is original.

I did not invent the concepts that follow. They are simply the wisdom that I have learned from my mentors who learned from their mentors, etc.

If you are picking up a tennis racket for the first time, this is not the book for you. It's not meant to be a how-to but rather a reminder of the key elements of strokes, strategy, and the mental game. Reminders that will truly make you a better player. If you have some experience but find your game at a standstill, this book will help you.

Parts 1–4 will move quickly. I'll go through key aspects of hitting the ball, strategy, and the mental game. In Part 5, I'll go a bit deeper on the topic of improvement. Each chapter stands on its own, so if you have an hour until your next appointment or five minutes before your next match, you'll find the book an easy read.

Throughout the book, I've sprinkled in quotes from other pros that I think you'll find helpful. At the end of the book, I've included a bonus section on doubles, the game played by most recreational players.

You might be thinking, with millions of tennis information sources available, does the world really need another tennis book? Read the book, commit to applying the concepts, and see how it goes. Then you can decide.

Part 1
Three Truths You Must Accept

Chapter 1
Nothing Will Work If You Don't

You need time, patience, and a strong ego to significantly improve your tennis. Time on the court to ingrain efficient techniques and strategies, patience for the lengthy (sometimes monotonous) process of learning, and a secure ego to endure the periodic failures you'll suffer along the way.

Time

How often do you play? If once a week is all you can manage, leave all performance expectations in the car. Enjoy the great days and brush aside the horrific ones—you'll have both. If you're a member of the four times a month club, look forward to your time on the court, get some exercise, and have fun.

If you can manage to play twice a week, that's great. You'll develop some consistency and see improvement over time. Three times a week is ideal: one lesson, one practice session, and one match. During the lesson, work on various techniques. In practice, incorporate those techniques into your game plan. On this schedule, you should enjoy steady improvement.

Patience

Once you're playing three or more times a week, you've made a legitimate commitment to becoming a better player. At this point, patience is a must. Many players have high expectations and expect quick results. It's not going to happen! Teaching pros are often asked how long it will take to get to the next level. Believe me, the pro has no idea. If they tell you they do, find a different pro.

Significant improvement takes time and is not a straight, upward path. Along the way, you'll sometimes feel as if you move ahead three steps and then drop back two. You must have patience with the process. Otherwise, you will not improve.

Secure Ego

As you work on your game, you're going to fail—a lot! Balls will hit every part of your racket but the strings. They'll fly to the side, sail up in the air, and sometimes they may even go backward.

You'll feel frustrated, uncoordinated, and perhaps worst of all, you'll think you look foolish in front of others. The ego is a fragile thing and failing in front of others is hard to handle. However, failure is a key element of improvement. Accept it and learn from it.

> *For many players, the pain of change is greater than the pain of losing.*
>
> **– Steve Smith**
> **Founder of GreatBase**
> **Tennis**

Of course, this is easier said than done. After your tenth serve in a row, with your new grip, hits the bottom of the net, your ego will scream things like:

> "This grip doesn't work."
> "My serve was better before."
> "My pro doesn't know what he's talking about."
> "I'm going back to my old grip."

Failure and ego are the adversaries of improvement. The truth is failure provides valuable information and opportunities to adjust and learn. The first hundred balls hit with a new grip or technique will feel horrible. If they don't, you're probably not doing it correctly. However, with every bad shot, you're one shot closer to mastering the technique.

As far as feeling foolish in front of others, trust me, no one's watching you. Many years ago, I found a great quote that sums it up perfectly:

> *People spend the first part of their lives worried about what others think about them.*
> *They spend the second part of their lives not caring what others think about them.*
> *Finally, they get to the point where they realize that no one's thinking about them because they're too busy thinking about themselves.*

Time, patience, and a secure ego. If, at this point in your life, you don't possess all three, significant improvement is not going to happen and that's OK. Have fun, get some exercise, and if you improve a little along the way, great. In a few years when the kids are grown, or you stop working, you might have more time to work on your tennis.

Until then, take an honest look at how much time you are able, or willing, to devote to your game and adjust your expectations accordingly.

Chapter 2
Trying to Play Like the Pros Is Ridiculous

Many years ago, I had the opportunity to play in an exhibition doubles match with Fred Stolle and Butch Buchholz. Stolle and Buchholz are two of the game's all-time greats, but at the time, they were 20 years past their prime and at least as many pounds above their playing weight. How good could they be?

Walking onto the court, the two old pros looked like your typical middle-aged, weekend warriors. Both possessed that too many hours on the court gait that's waiting for us all in the third set of our lives. They also wore the requisite equipment for aging athletes: braces, straps, and tape on their elbows, knees, and ankles. I was young, fit, and ready to show the "old guys" how the game was played in the modern era.

We began to warm up and, suddenly, the "old guys" didn't seem so old. Their posture straightened, their step quickened, and they struck the ball with a consistency I'd never seen. They hit shots that landed within six inches of the baseline and had the control of a concert maestro. After two games, I hid in my tiny corner of the court, praying that the ball wouldn't come near me. I'd been served up a true dose of tennis reality.

It was on that day I realized that tennis, as it's played at the professional level, bears such little resemblance to the sport that the majority of us play, that comparisons are far and few between.

When you watch a professional tennis player, you're seeing a finished product, someone who has spent thousands of hours hitting millions of balls to fully develop their very special talent. As a result, they're able to brilliantly and consistently execute techniques that require extraordinary timing.

Today's pros use grips, stances, and employ jarring shoulder and hip rotations designed to generate more racket head speed. With so many moving parts, the pros need—and have developed—superb timing and athleticism to consistently hit the ball cleanly. The average player does not possess these skills.

Furthermore, our bodies are not built to viciously rotate hundreds of times during each match. These jolting movements put tremendous pressure on our joints, which can ultimately lead to a breakdown. I've seen many recreational and junior players develop injuries as a result of their attempts to execute the modern techniques because they simply do not possess the physical strength, flexibility, or coordination of the pros.

This is not meant as a putdown of the recreational player but rather a reality check. To imitate the pro's approach to striking the ball is a waste of time. It will not help your game and can potentially hurt you.

Does this mean there's nothing we can learn from watching the pros play? Absolutely not! It's fun to watch and marvel at the best in the world. The pros do it themselves.

Roger Federer regularly watched other players to pick up their tactics and techniques. Serena Williams did as well—only, according to her former coach Patrick Mouratoglou, "Serena watched a ton of men's tennis. Never women."

> *99.99% of the people who ever pick up a racket will never play on the pro tour. So why are people trying to learn to play like that?*
>
> **– Brent Abel**
> **Founder of Web Tennis**

The next time you watch a professional match, ignore how they hold and swing their rackets. Instead, pay attention to these 10 things.

1. **How they warm up.** They hit focused groundstrokes and then move forward to hit volleys and overheads. After that, they move back for serves. Yes, they've likely hit for 30–40 minutes before taking the court to loosen up and break a sweat (you should as well) but they still make good use of those final ten minutes to prepare for the match.

2. **Their feet**. Notice their split steps, the way they change direction, and how (and where) they recover after hitting their shots.

3. **Their early racket preparation**. Go to YouTube and watch videos of Venus and Serena. Nobody does it better.

4. **Their return of serve.** The pros rarely try to win the point with one swing of their racket. Their plan is to return the serve and then develop the point.

5. **Their overall consistency.** The player (or team) that commits the fewest errors wins the match virtually every time.

6. **How big their shot targets are as opposed to going for the lines.** Big targets mean fewer errors.

7. **Their rituals.** See Rafael Nadal or Maria Sharapova.

8. **Their effort**. No one has ever tried harder on a tennis court than Rafael Nadal and Jimmy Connors.

9. **Their ability to reset after losing a set.** Novak Djokovic is the best.

10. **Emotions.** Whether you're playing in the US Open final or a USTA 3.0 match, whenever the score is being kept, emotions can run high. Pay attention to how the pros handle their emotions on the court. Federer and Rafael Nadal win by keeping their emotions under control; Novak Djokovic and Serena Williams win by letting them out. Find which works for you.

Chapter 3
Hitting Winners Will Not Win Matches

Many players believe that, to move to the higher levels of the game, they need to learn how to finish points quickly by hitting winners. "Hit big to win big" is the mantra. As a result, these players develop the disease of "more."

They want to hit with **more** power, **more** spin or **more** angle because they believe it will allow them to hit **more** winners. These players couldn't be **more** wrong! The disease of "more" brings more errors, more losses, and often more injuries.

The truth is tennis is not a game of winners. It's a game of errors. In fact, at the professional level, errors outnumber winners by more than ten to one. At the recreational level, that number balloons to thirty to one. Accepting this is your first step toward becoming a better tennis player.

Understanding Errors

There are two types of errors, forced and unforced. A forced error is caused by an opponent's shot that's simply too tough to handle. An unforced error is a careless mistake that had absolutely nothing to do with anything your opponent did.

At the 3.5 level and below, the majority of errors are unforced. As players improve and develop a greater command of their strokes and strategy, forced errors begin to outnumber unforced mistakes. In other words, better players commit fewer unforced errors.

What causes errors? As I said, forced errors are caused by your opponent's strong shots. There's not much you can do except try to avoid creating situations where your opponent can press you, such as hitting short balls, high volleys, and weak second serves.

Unforced errors are primarily caused by a lapse in focus. Our mind wanders, we get sloppy with our technique, or more frequently, we select the wrong shot. The vast majority of unforced errors simply come from trying low-percentage shots, typically shots with too much power or placement and too little net clearance.

Instead of approaching your path to improvement with the strategy of "more," become a better player by doing less—but doing it better. Learn to minimize your unforced errors and design strategies that force your opponents to miss. The first step is to commit to becoming a more consistent player.

You will never be a high-level tennis player if you can't keep the ball in play. Consistency is largely a mind-set, so the next time you play, do so with a refuse to miss attitude. If you can hit the ball in the court five times each point, you'll likely beat 90% of the players who are beating you now.

Here are two strategies that will immediately make you a more consistent player.

1. **Aim higher over the net.** Clearing the net is your first obstacle, so develop three different heights with which you can hit your groundstrokes. First is a rally height (4–6 feet over the net) for when you're in a baseline exchange and no one has the advantage. Next is a defensive height (15–20 feet over the net) used when you're in trouble. Finally, develop an offensive height (1–2 feet over the net) for when you are attacking a short ball or hitting a passing shot.

2. **Stay away from the lines**. Never, ever aim for the lines! Australian coaching legend Harry Hopman was famous for telling his players to "hit for the lines." With all due respect to "Hop," I say that unless your name is Laver, Williams, or Federer, forget about the lines. Play it safe and always aim 1-2 feet inside the lines.

Great Shot, Don't Do It Again

These words fly out of my mouth after one of my players hits what they view to be a great shot. You know—a desperation forehand that barely kisses the line, or a sharply angled ball that skims the net and lands two inches from the sideline.

Shots like these are exciting to see, exhilarating to execute, and the response they draw from other players feels awesome. They drop their rackets, clap their hands, and bow to the player's greatness.

Everyone loves praise so the player tries to recapture that magic moment. They continue to go for the low-percentage, jaw-dropping shot, which almost always, results in a stream of impressive-looking errors. They end up hitting a few outstanding shots but lose the match.

The truth is these "great" shots aren't great at all. They're lucky and trying to recreate them is a recipe for disaster. The next time you walk onto a court, take ten balls, drop them one at a time, pick a line across the net, and try to hit it. Or try to hit a sharply angled ball that skims the net and brushes the doubles sideline. How many times out of ten can you do it? One, two, maybe three, if you're particularly skilled.

If you can execute these "great" shots only twenty percent of the time, in a no-pressure situation, what does that say about your chances of hitting them under the fast-paced pressure of a match? It says that when you do it, you're lucky and lucky does not win matches.

Part 2
The Truth About Hitting the Ball

Tennis strokes are just not that complicated. They can't be. Consider all that's going on. The ball's moving, your racket's moving, and you're moving. That's a lot of moving parts to bring together to achieve your primary technical goal—solid contact between your strings and the ball.

Always remember that there is no right or wrong way to hold or swing a tennis racket. However, there is an efficient and a less efficient way. If you have grips, stances, and stroking patterns that require tremendous coordination, adjustments and timing, there's huge potential for a breakdown from split step to contact. With efficient mechanics, there are fewer things that can go wrong.

The key to effective shot making lies in a few fundamentals that focus on anticipation, preparation, efficiency, and solid contact. This becomes increasingly important as you reach the 4.0 level where the game becomes much faster.

> *Cut out the fancy thinking and just concentrate on mastering the fundamentals, and you'll beat most of the players who beat you now.*
>
> **– Vic Braden**
> **Tennis Teaching Legend**

As you move through the next few pages, you'll undoubtedly be tempted to skip ahead, thinking, "Yeah, I know this." That would be a mistake. Knowing and doing are two very different things.

Chapter 4
It All Starts Here

If you want to immediately take your strokes to the next level, improve your ready position and master the split step.

Do not turn the page!

The ready position and split step are two of those "Yeah, I know" areas of the game that players tend to push aside for what they believe to be more important training. The truth is to play high-level tennis, you must learn a proper ready position and you must make the split step a habit. Without both,

> *Everything starts with the ready position.*
>
> – **Nick Bollettieri**
> **Tennis Teaching Legend**

you'll be late moving to the ball, struggle with balance, and your strokes will break down. I guarantee it.

Teaching pros do their students a great disservice when they don't stress these two techniques. I admit that, for many years, I was guilty of it myself. I'd briefly go over the ready position and split step but quickly move on to backswing and follow-through. They're more fun because the player's actually hitting the ball.

Plus, at the beginner and advanced beginner levels, the ball's moving slowly and doesn't come back very often. A player can get away with a casual ready position and doesn't need the quick start the split step provides. As a result, he develops sloppy preparation habits that ultimately catch up to him.

At the 4.0 level and above, tennis changes dramatically. The ball comes back more frequently and it's moving much faster. With the proper ready position and split step, these changes won't seem so drastic. You'll be able to easily make grip changes, properly prepare your racket, move to the ball quickly, and swing your racket efficiently.

The Ready Position

Keep in mind that the ready position is not just the position you take while waiting to receive serve. It's the position you should return to after every shot you hit.

Follow these steps to be truly prepared for your next shot.

1. Face the net.
2. As most players hit more forehands than backhands, wait with your right (bottom) hand holding your forehand grip.
3. If you have a two-handed backhand, your left hand should be on top of (but not overlapping) your right. Also, with a forehand grip.
4. For players with a one-handed backhand, the non-dominant hand can be placed higher on the throat of the racket for stability.
5. Your racket hand should be at waist height.
6. Spread your feet shoulder width apart with your toes pointing forward.
7. Bend your knees slightly and lean forward with your weight on the balls of your feet.
8. Your head is still with your eyes looking over the tip of your racket.
9. Your upper body should be relaxed and your back straight.
10. Your arms should be away from your body and elbows slightly raised. A junior player should be able to drop a volleyball between his elbows. An adult, a basketball.

The Split Step

The secret to the split step lies in the timing. If you hop too soon, you'll be off-balance when your opponent strikes his shot. If you hop late, you'll be late reacting. Pay close attention to your opponent's racket. As it begins to move forward toward the ball, bend your knees and hop into the air.

Time the hop so that you're in the air as the ball is struck. As you come down (and have determined which direction the ball is traveling) using an explosive push, turn your body toward the ball and begin moving. The higher off the ground you hop, the more force you'll apply with your feet to the court when you land, making your first step more explosive.

You may initially struggle with the timing, but you'll soon find that you're reacting much faster and able to prepare for your shots much more efficiently.

The next time you play, commit to taking a split step before every shot your opponent (or practice partner) hits. A good training tool is to actually say the word "split" at the appropriate time to remind yourself to split step.

In addition to enabling you to react faster, the split step will help you stay mentally alert. I often find that when my feet get lazy, my mind wanders—and vice versa. When I remind myself to be up on my toes and take strong split steps, my focus and level of play improve tremendously.

Chapter 5
The Keys to Anticipation

Wouldn't it be great if you knew where your opponent was going to hit his next shot before he actually hit it? It would certainly make executing your own strokes a lot easier.

High-level players, to a large extent, can do this. They've learned to anticipate their opponent's shots, and as a result, are able to begin their preparation sooner and ultimately execute balanced, confident shots.

Keep in mind that anticipation is not about knowing exactly where your opponent's going to hit every ball—that's impossible. Instead, it's about narrowing the number of possibilities he has to the one or two most likely.

To develop your anticipation skills, you'll need to break the cardinal rule of tennis: Watch the ball. Once you've completed your shot, watching the ball provides little information as to what's coming next. Instead, shift your eyes from your contact point to your opponent. Look for things such as:

> *Keep your eyes glues to your opponent. You must practice watching him closely as you move in order to become sensitive to the small clues which will give away the direction of his next shot.*
>
> **– Allen Fox**
> **Author of *Think to Win***

- **Position.** Where is he standing on the court?
- **Movement.** Is he moving forward, backward, or diagonally?
- **Body language.** Is he balanced or off-balance?
- **Swing.** Is he taking a large or small backswing?
- **Strike zone.** Where is the ball relative to his body?

With this information, you'll be able to anticipate, with a high rate of success, your opponent's next shot. For example, if you see he's moving back behind the baseline, and the ball is above his shoulders, he's on defense.

From this position, you can expect him to hit a high ball, probably crosscourt. Take a step or two inside the baseline and the moment he strikes the ball, move forward and look to attack. If he's balanced and moving forward, he's likely to hit an aggressive shot. Buy yourself some time by backing up a step or two. Here are a few more things to look for:

- If he's hitting his groundstrokes with a closed stance (stepping across his body), there's a good chance he'll be hitting down the line.
- If he's lining up with an open stance, chest pointing toward the net, his body will have more natural rotation. Look for a cross-court ball.
- If his racket face is open, he's likely going to hit a high shot or one with slice. If his racket face is closed, he'll usually be hitting a low ball or one with topspin.
- If he's hitting late, he'll likely hit down the line.
- If his backswing looks higher than usual, anticipate a drop shot.
- If he takes a big backswing, prepare for a hard shot. A shorter backswing, a softer, shorter ball.
- When your opponent is serving, you can often anticipate where the serve will go by looking at his toss. For example, if the toss is behind his head he'll likely hit a high-bouncing, topspin serve. If the toss is out to the side of his hitting-arm, anticipate a low-bouncing slice serve.

Also, pay attention to your opponent's tendencies. In certain situations, most players will hit the same shot virtually every time—it's what makes them most comfortable. Recognizing and remembering their tendencies will come in very handy, particularly when the big points arrive.

When You Give Your Opponent a Sitter

When a high-level player has time to prepare, all bets are off. Your anticipation will be more of an educated guess. You'll need to make a quick decision and commit to moving to one side or the other before they strike the ball—otherwise, you'll never be able to catch up to their shot.

The next time your opponent is preparing to take a big swing (e.g., for a short groundstroke, floating volley, or easy overhead), his momentum and natural path of his racket will tend to pull the ball crosscourt. In these situations, guess crosscourt until he shows you otherwise.

Chapter 6
Sight and Sound

From a technical standpoint, the relationship between your eyes and the tennis ball is just as important as the one between your hand and your racket. When you learn to properly see the ball, you'll be more relaxed, prepare more efficiently, and execute your strokes with more confidence. The next time you play, try this approach to watching the ball.

1. **Scan**. When the ball leaves your opponent's racket, scan for the direction (left or right) the ball will be traveling. This will tell you whether you'll be hitting a forehand or backhand.
2. **Track**. As the ball travels toward you, track it as you move into position.
3. **Focus.** When the ball has bounced and is moving toward you (approximately the last 3 feet), deepen your focus. We've all heard the tip to "see the ball hit your strings." The ball is on your strings for 3-6 milliseconds. To actually see the ball hit the strings is impossible. Instead, look for the spin on the ball as it approaches.

The Moment of Truth

With every shot you hit, your initial goal is to create controlled, solid contact between your strings and the ball. When you strike the ball, keep your eyes fixed on your point of contact.

> *When you move your own head, you disturb the flight pattern of your racquet head.*
>
> *– Vic Braden*

Lenny Schloss, the founder and president of Billie Jean King's Eye Coach (a fabulous training aid), says that "Eighty percent of all mishits are caused by our eyes shifting off the point of contact too soon."

When your eyes shift, your head moves as well. When this happens, your racket head shifts, leading to mishits and a loss of control. Keeping your head and eyes on the point of contact after you strike the ball will help ensure solid contact. How long should you keep it there? For one recovery step. Then you can look up and begin preparing for your next shot.

Triple Vision

The scan, track, and focus progression, along with holding your eyes on the point of contact, will immediately help you hit technically stronger shots. From a tactical standpoint, you need to develop what's known as triple vision.

When a quarterback drops back to pass, he's aware of his position on the field as well as where his teammates and opponents are. When a point guard in basketball, a center in hockey, or a midfielder in soccer move forward, they have the same awareness. This skill is called triple vision.

As you play, work on broadening the scope of your focus from simply the ball to your opponent and the court. With every shot you hit, you need to be aware of where you are on the court, where your opponent is, and of course, where the ball is. This will play a major role in your shot selection. Here are three examples of triple vision:

- You're receiving serve from the deuce court during a doubles match. The serve pulls you out wide. As you move to hit your return, you're focused on the ball. However, in your field of vision, you also see that the opposing net player hasn't shifted to cover his alley, leaving you with a huge opening to end the point with a down the line return.
- During a singles match, your opponent hits a drop shot. As you charge forward, you see that he's not moved forward. All you need to do is return the drop shot with one of your own and the point should be yours.
- You're moving forward to attack a short, high forehand. As you approach the ball, you notice that your opponent moves to his right, anticipating that you'll go crosscourt. Recognizing this, you hit the ball down the line into the open court.

A great drill for practicing triple vision is to grab a partner and play mini tennis—using two balls. You feed each other a ball at the same time and try to keep both balls going.

While you're focusing on executing your shots, you'll also have to develop an awareness of the other ball. This exercise will also improve your footwork. With two balls in play, you'll have to immediately begin moving for the next ball. Once you master the drill up close, move back to the baseline and do the same.

Don't Forget to Listen

Listening to the ball is rarely discussed but is a vital aspect of preparing for an opponent's shots. Tennis legend Jimmy Connors once commented he hated to play when he had a cold because he couldn't hear the ball coming off of his opponent's racket.

Learn to recognize the type of sound the ball makes when it hits your opponent's strings. It will help you determine how hard or soft the ball has been hit, if it's been hit with excessive spin, or if it's been mishit. Each has its own distinctive voice.

A hard-hit ball sounds like a big boom, while a ball hit softly sounds more like a tap. A ball hit with excessive spin makes a hissing sound and a mishit shot bears that unmistakable clunk.

By watching, and listening, to the ball, you'll pick up vital cues as to where your opponent's shot is going to bounce and what it's going to do after it lands. You can then respond accordingly.

For example, if you see that the ball is traveling three feet or more above the net and sounds as if it's been hit hard (boom), you need to back up—ASAP. Conversely, if the ball comes off your opponent's racket with a trajectory lower than two feet over the net and the sound is softer (tap), quickly move forward because the ball will likely land short in your court.

If you hear the sound of spin (hiss) and your opponent has swung with a low to high motion, he's hit with topspin. The ball will pick up speed after it lands which means you'll need to prepare faster. If you hear the hiss and the swing was a high-to-low motion, that means slice, which will cause the ball to stay low after it hits the court.

If your opponent mishits his shot (clunk), it's very difficult to determine which way the ball will jump after it bounces. Try to move forward and hit it in the air so you won't have to deal with the unpredictable bounce. If you can't reach the ball in time, get to the spot where you anticipate it will land and expect a crazy bounce. Shorten your backswing, and most of the time, you'll be able to react quickly enough to get the ball back in play with a solid shot.

Chapter 7
Balance Is Everything

Teaching pros speak endlessly about the intricacies of footwork. We talk about different footwork patterns and techniques, such as the "drop step," the "front cross-over recovery step," and the "forward hit and hop." Some even paint feet onto the court as paths for their students to follow. It all sounds very impressive and makes us appear very educated and cutting edge. In the world of recreational tennis, it's also largely useless!

I realized this one day watching a USTA doubles match. As I saw the players sprinting, stretching, and straining to get to the ball, I knew the last thing on their minds was which foot should go where. That's when I began emphasizing balance to my players—and the improvement has been dramatic.

When your body is balanced, your mind calms, you relax, and you're able to execute controlled strokes and strategy. The moment you lose your balance, your mind falls into panic mode, and the ability to control your body and racket face disappears.

The next time you play, forget about footwork and focus on balance. Yes, footwork is important. However, view it as a tool to gain and maintain your balance, and the truth is much of that happens automatically.

> *Balance helps shape the stroke. It involves the feet, hips, head, and non-racket arm. Balance is the picture frame in which the picture (the stroke) is placed.*
>
> **– Welby Van Horn**
> **Tennis Teaching Legend**

How often do you see someone actually fall over on the tennis court? Rarely. That's because our bodies naturally want to be in balance.

Go to any tennis court in the world and you'll see people scrambling around the court as if they're auditioning for Cirque du Soleil. Their upper body is going one way, their lower another. Their arms are flapping like wings, and their faces display expressions of utter panic. The reason: They've lost their balance and the various contortions are their bodies' natural way of trying to regain it.

Your body is in balance when your belly button (your center of gravity) is over your base, your feet, which should be roughly a racket's distance apart. If your belly button moves outside of that base, you're off-balance.

As you move closer to the ball, shorten your steps. This will help you both fine-tune your positioning and maintain your balance. A great way to create better balance is to simply bend your knees. Doing so will lower your center of gravity. This will give you a more stable base. Many players make the mistake of bending from their waist when they begin to move toward a ball. As a result, they immediately put their bodies out of balance.

Learn to use your non-dominant hand to improve your balance. You're holding a racket on one side of your body, so you need something to counter-balance your body on the other side. Your non-dominant arm is it.

When hitting a forehand groundstroke, point at the on-coming ball with your non-racket hand. Not only will this help you to balance, but it's also a great tool to track the approaching ball. If you hit a one-handed backhand, as your right arm goes forward, push your left arm back. This will keep you balanced as well as prevent your shoulders from opening up. Your left arm also helps you to balance when hitting volleys, overheads, and serves.

Become aware of when you're balanced, when you're not, and adjust your shot selection accordingly. If, as you prepare to swing your racket, you feel balanced—and the situation warrants it—hit an aggressive ball. However, if you feel off-balance in any way, push aside those "I can do it" thoughts of greatness and simply put the ball back in play.

Remember, if one or both of your feet are off the ground, you're not balanced. The pros can maintain their balance when they leave the ground—you and I cannot.

Here's a great exercise to help you become more aware of the balance factor: drop the ball and hit it. Don't worry about where the ball goes. Instead, try to comfortably freeze after each shot. If you can, you've likely executed a balanced stroke. If you can't, you've lost your balance. To progress from this, try to do the same when you rally—freeze for a brief moment after you've completed your follow-through.

Chapter 8
Space and Time(ing)

To execute balanced strokes, you must create the proper amount of space between your body and the ball. Doing so will allow you to step forward, rotate your shoulders and move your racket through the hitting zone.

In my experience, being positioned too close to the ball is, without question, the most common mistake recreational players make. They start moving late, and in their panic to make up for lost time, end up running right into the ball. As a result, they lose their balance and their stroke falls apart.

The moment you come down from your split step, immediately turn your shoulders and begin moving toward the ball. Your goal is to get into the general area where the ball will bounce as quickly as possible. If you have a long distance to travel (12 feet or more), take bigger steps. For a shorter distance, use shuffle steps.

As you approach the ball, shorten those steps. This will help you fine-tune your positioning, balance your body, and calculate the proper amount of space between you and the ball.

Once you've arrived, and are properly spaced, your next task is to time the shot so you can make contact with the ball in your ideal strike zone. Teaching pros have varying numbers of strike zones, I have three:

Strike zone #1: below your knees
Strike zone # 2: from your knees to chest
Strike zone #3: above your chest

Striking the ball in zone 2 should be your goal. In this zone your shoulders, hip, torso, and legs can propel your racket for power, while your arm and wrist control your racket face. In zones 1 and 3, you're forced to recruit the muscles in your arm to move your racket and generate pace. When this happens, your technique can easily break down.

On high balls, position yourself five to six feet behind the bounce and wait for the ball to drop into zone 2. On low shots, again, position yourself behind the ball and bend your knees so that you can make contact as close to zone 2 as possible.

Your goal, with every shot in the game, is to step forward and make contact with the ball in front of your body.

To develop zone awareness, the next time you practice, call out the zones of every ball before you swing your racket. Ideally, you're saying "zone 2" quite a bit. If not, you likely need to work harder on your footwork to get to a better position.

Chapter 9
Shoulders, Palms, and Knuckles

Bring your racket back this way, follow through that way, use a big loop, a small loop, no loop, elbow in, elbow out, wrist up, wrist down. There are more theories about stroke mechanics than there are flavors at Ben & Jerry's.

Forget about backswing and follow-through. Instead focus on your shoulders, palm, and knuckles. These are the only mechanics you'll need.

Shoulders

Once you've taken your split step and determined where your opponent's shot is going, immediately turn your shoulders to the side of the oncoming ball. This shoulder turn (called the "unit turn") combined with the proper ready position previously discussed—will move your racket into the correct position.

Think of your shoulders, arms, torso and hips as one unit with your priority being to minimize arm, wrist, and racket head movement. The shoulder turn is your first move for every shot in the game—the only thing that will vary is how much you turn. Follow these general guidelines:

On groundstrokes when you have time. Fully turn your shoulders so that your opponent can see your back. For comparison purposes, we'll call this a 100% turn. Most players don't turn their shoulders nearly enough. Steve Smith – tennis coaching legend – says, "Turn too much to turn enough."

On groundstrokes when you're pressured. Turn 50%.

On volleys when you have time. Turn 50%. You should always be able to see your racket out of the corner of your eye.

On volleys when pressured. Think less about turning and more about moving your hand and racket forward to absorb the incoming ball.

On overheads with time. 100% turn.

On overheads when pressured. Turn 50% and turn the overhead into a volley. Simply push it back (like a high five) and begin preparing for your next shot.

Just as you turn your shoulders to prepare your racket, you'll rotate them forward to move your racket to strike the ball. Again, there should be little, if any, movement in your arm, elbow, or wrist. Think of your shoulders and hips as the engine that drives the racket and your arm and hand as the steering wheel that directs your shots.

Palm and Knuckles

To control the direction of your shots, all you need to remember is that the ball is going to go where your strings are pointed at the moment of impact. The ball hits your strings for 3-6 milliseconds. This is when it receives its orders: Crosscourt, down the line, high, low, speed up, slow down, topspin, or slice. The ball has no idea what style of grip, backswing, or follow-through you have. All it knows is the position, path, and speed of your racket face.

Focus on controlling your racket face at impact. This is best done by thinking of your racket face as an extension of your hand. As your hand moves, so moves your racket face. Keep your wrist firm so that your wrist and racket head move together. When your wrist is firm, you're much better able to feel and control the face of your racket. For a firm wrist, squeeze your grip with your bottom three fingers just before impact. These are the fingers that connect to the tendons that tighten and loosen your wrist.

When hitting a forehand, focus on the palm of your racket hand. The face of your racket (and the ball) will go where your palm goes. If you use an extreme western grip, you'll need to adjust your wrist in order to make contact with the ball with your strings pointing toward your target. If you have a two-handed backhand, focus on the palm of your top hand. If you use a one-handed backhand, use your knuckles to guide the face of your racket.

Always keep your primary focus on pointing your strings toward your target. Vary your contact point depending upon where you want to hit your shot. To hit crosscourt, make contact further in front of your body. For down-the-line shots, still strike the ball in front of your body, only not as far.

A great way to develop this "feel" between your hand and racket face is to play mini tennis. With a much smaller court area, you can't hit the ball hard and keep it in play, so there is virtually no backswing or follow-through. As a result, you can deeply focus on your hand and how it relates to your strings.

Follow-Through and Finish

When I ask players how to direct the ball, they frequently reply "with my follow-through." Well, by the time you feel the ball hit your strings, it's already traveled seven to eleven feet away from you. By the time you follow through, the ball is long gone.

However, the follow-through does help your racket stay on a long, smooth and precise forward path. Focus on a long follow-through where your strings remain pointing toward your target for as long as possible. To help with this, imagine swinging through three balls, one right after the other. After you make contact with the first ball, keep your racket moving forward as if you were hitting two more balls on the same path. You'll be surprised how solid, accurate, and consistent your shots become.

After you've struck the ball, keep your eyes on your point of contact for one recovery step and continue rotating your shoulders forward until your racket points to your target. Then, simply decelerate and relax your arm, letting your racket finish over your shoulder.

The Toughest Shot in Tennis Is...the Next One!

Once you've finished your shot, immediately begin preparing for the next. If you've hit a ball 12 feet or less from the center of the baseline, recover using shuffle steps. This will keep you facing your opponent and allow you to easily move in any direction.

On balls when you're pulled very wide, recover by using one or two explosive crossover steps (bring your outside leg over your inside as you move laterally back toward the center). The crossover steps will help you get back into the court faster. Then, move to shuffle steps. As your opponent prepares to hit their next shot, be ready to split step.

Chapter 10
Dealing with Awkward Shots

In the Introduction, I wrote that I would not be offering a lot of technical instruction. However, there are a few shots that I see players struggle with on a daily basis. With that in mind, I'd like to give you a few strategies for dealing with four of the game's most awkward shots.

The Half Volley

A half volley (or pick-up) is that difficult shot you have to play when a ball bounces right at your feet. You can't move forward quickly enough to hit the ball in the air, and it bounces too fast and close to your body to execute a proper groundstroke.

Players usually get trapped into playing a half volley when they approach the net and the ball is driven at their feet. Or occasionally, they'll get caught standing inside their baseline when their opponent drives a fast, deep ball right at them.

Your goals with a half volley are to get the ball back in play and as deep as possible. Use an extremely short shoulder turn and keep your racket out in front of you. Be sure your wrist is firm and bend your knees to lower yourself to the level of the ball.

As soon as the ball hits the ground, keep your racket face square or slightly open and gently lift the ball over the net. Your motion should be more of a push than a swing. Stay low and use a slight, I repeat slight, upward motion. Be sure your head stays down and your eyes remain on your point of contact after striking the ball.

Above all, do not try to be aggressive when hitting a half volley. Get the ball back in play and then move into the net or back behind the baseline so you won't have to hit another one.

A good exercise to practice the timing of a half volley is to say the words "boom boom" (like a heartbeat) to yourself as fast as you can when hitting the shot. This will give you a feel for the rhythm involved and improve your timing.

The Backhand Overhead

Few will argue that the backhand overhead is one of the most technically challenging shots in tennis. It's awkward to position for and (with your neck and back turned away from the net) difficult to maintain good eye contact with the ball. Plus, the muscles needed to hit a backhand overhead are not the ones used to hit most other shots in the game. As a result, they're weaker which makes it more difficult to control your shot.

Assuming you can't quickly move around the ball and hit your regular overhead, turn the shot into a volley. Turn your shoulders and, like a volley, keep your racket in front of your body. Using the front of your racket hand as guidance for your strings, focus on keeping your head still and making solid contact with the ball. Push the ball back over the net with high clearance. Your target should be deep into your opponent's backcourt.

Right at You

How often have you been at the net and your opponent drives the ball right at you? This happens quite frequently, particularly in doubles, and is in fact an excellent strategy that often handcuffs the net player.

Ideally, when a ball is coming right at your body, try to move to one side or the other so you can comfortably play either a forehand or backhand volley. If you don't have the time to move, keep your wrist firm and play a backhand volley. That's really the only way you can physically get the racket in front of your body without severely (and dangerously) contorting your arm. Keep your wrist firm and just let the ball hit your strings.

The Over-the-Shoulder Shot

A lob flies over your head and you immediately know you're in trouble. There's no way you'll be able to hit the ball in the air, and you won't have time to run behind it and hit a controlled groundstroke. You're going to have to hit the shot in front of your body with your back to the net. Now what?

As you sprint back, position yourself so that when the ball bounces, it's over your left shoulder. As you swing your racket, imagine that you're going to throw the racket over your left shoulder. Using a continental grip, "flick" your wrist to generate more power.

In this very defensive position, your best tactic is to swing upward and return the ball with a high lob to stay in the point. If your lob lands deep, you may even win the point.

Chapter 11
Use Spin to Win

Hitting with spin will enhance your consistency, control, and creativity. When you hit with topspin, you can make the ball bounce extremely high, and there's not a player in the world who likes to hit balls above their shoulder, particularly on his backhand side. When you hit with slice, you force your opponent to bend low and hit up. Again, something no player enjoys.

Topspin

A ball hit with topspin will initially rise and then, very quickly, fall. This allows you to swing harder, aim higher, yet still keep the ball in the court. When the ball bounces on the other side of the net, the spin will cause it to accelerate, making your opponent feel as if it's jumping right on top of them. Think of topspin as your power spin.

A common instruction for hitting topspin is to imagine hitting over the ball. Let's think about that: If you bring your racket face over the ball, your strings will be on top of it. Is the ball then going to come up through the strings to get over the net? I don't think so. Forget hitting over the ball.

To add topspin to your shots, your racket must be below your point of contact at the start of your swing and above the contact point at the finish. As you prepare, drop your racket approximately 12 inches below the height of the ball. Do this by bending your knees, not dropping your arm or wrist.

Then, as you step forward, lift your legs and rotate your shoulders and hips. This will bring your racket to the contact point. Your hips, shoulders, and racket should be aligned and moving as one unit. Think of the motion as upward and forward.

If the ball were the face of a clock, topspin rotation would bring 6 over 12 as the ball moves away from you.

When to Hit with Topspin

1. **Most of the time when you're in a baseline rally.** Topspin gives you a greater margin for error. Plus, when you hit deep with topspin, your ball bounces higher, creating an awkward shot for your opponent.
2. **When you want to be aggressive.** A well-hit ball with topspin will move quickly through the air and bounce very fast, taking time away from your opponent.
3. **When your opponent is at the net.** Balls hit with topspin will drop after crossing the net, forcing him to react faster as well as bend more at the knees.

When Not to Hit with Topspin

1. **On approach shots.** When moving forward to attack a short ball, it's easy to get overly excited and run right into the ball.

If you struggle with this, forget topspin and hit your approach shots with slice. Slice is easier to hit on the run and gives you more time to move to the net. Also, the low bounce will make it extremely challenging for your opponent to hit an effective passing shot.

2. **On very low balls.** Low shots are difficult to get your racket sufficiently beneath the ball to return with topspin. Instead, slice it back and wait for something a little higher that you can attack with topspin.
3. **When returning a big serve.** You often won't have time to take a full swing to hit with topspin. Instead, block your return and get the point started. Roger Federer did this frequently.

Slice

Slice is produced by moving your racket from high to low and with a long follow through. As you prepare, your racket should be approximately six inches above the height of the ball and your arm bent like the letter 'L'. This will allow you to you to extend out through the contact point and use your triceps muscle for added power and stability.

As you step into the shot, rotate your shoulders, leading with the bottom edge of your racket. This will help you keep the racket moving in a downward motion as well as ensure that the racket is tilted up at a slight angle. Continue moving your racket down, forward, and then up at the end. Think of the shape of a banana. Staying with the clock analogy, slice rotation would bring 12 over 6 as the ball travels away from you.

When you slice the ball well, it will stay below your opponent's knees, making it very difficult for him to hit aggressively with topspin—particularly if they use a semi-western or western grip.

Plus, a ball hit with slice will travel through the air slower than one hit flat or with topspin, making it great for approach shots where you need time to get to the net as soon as you can. Think of slice as your finesse spin.

When to Hit with Slice

1. **To change pace.** During an intense topspin rally, mixing in a deep, low slice is a great tactic. The ball will slow down (which will give you a bit of a physical break) and bounce low, forcing your opponent to bend and hit up.

2. **To bring your opponent forward.** This is great when you're facing one of those players who loves to stay at the baseline and hates coming to the net. Hitting a short slice or drop shot will force him forward. When you do this, be sure to move forward as well.

If you hit the shot well, your opponent will be scrambling to reach it and will likely return your shot with a high ball that has little or no pace—easy for you to attack.

3. **When returning a fast serve.** You'll rarely have time to take a full swing on your return. Instead take advantage of your opponent's pace and, with a short backswing, block the ball back with slice deep into the court. Or, if he's charging the net, slice your return down at his feet.

4. **When you see that your opponent struggles to return it.** Most recreational players wait for the ball to come to them after it bounces. Because a ball hit with slice produces a low bounce, by the time the ball reaches them, it's often so low they're not able to get under it to hit a topspin return. Furthermore, many players hate to bend their knees so they'll often return your slice with another slice that sits up and has little pace.

When Not to Slice

1. **When you're deep in the court and the ball is at or above your head.** Instead, aim high over the net and roll the ball back with topspin.
2. **When you're on your back foot and can't transfer your weight forward.** Again, put the ball back in play with medium-paced topspin.
3. **When your opponent is at the net.** A ball hit with slice, if not hit perfectly, will tend to rise and float. If you've developed a feel for slice, you can hit a soft, low, slice at the net player's feet, but that's a difficult shot to execute under pressure. Typically, the only slice you should use in this situation is the slice lob.

Give It Time to Develop

Keep in mind that there are varying degrees of spin. The angle of your racket face at the moment of impact will determine its trajectory. Every adjustment of your racket face (palms and knuckles) will produce a different result.

Trial and error will help you develop the proper feel so that you can put as much (or as little) spin on the ball as you like. As you practice, remember to keep your wrist firm but flexible.

Don't panic when your initial attempts at hitting topspin hit you in the foot or your first slice backhand goes backward. Both will likely happen, and it's all part of the learning process.

With practice, you'll develop the appropriate feel and your game will move to an entirely new level!

Chapter 12
Adding Power the Correct Way

I often like to say that power is the last resort of the unskilled player. Players who haven't taken the time—or have the patience—to develop a disciplined approach to their tennis.

They step onto the court and blast away because they can't do anything else. They hit the occasional amazing shot, lose a lot of matches, but hey, at least they look good because they hit so hard.

I can honestly tell you that I have never said to a player, "Today, we're going to work on power." I don't believe you work on power. Power develops naturally as technique improves.

Simply put, power is gained by increased racket head speed. The problem is, when the average player hears the phrase "racket head speed," he equates it to swinging harder. He grips his racket a little tighter, clenches his jaw, and swings for the fences.

While this approach does move their racket faster, it also creates tension throughout the body. When this happens, the fluidity and control of the stroke disappear.

Yes, you need to increase the speed of your racket head as it makes contact with the ball. However, this should be done by coordinating movements of your legs, hip, trunk, shoulders, and arms so that they work together to propel your racket into the ball. This coordination is called the kinetic chain, and it means simply using the different links in the chain to sequentially transfer energy from one part of your body to the other.

Let's say you wanted to add power to your forehand. Wait for a ball that's in your ideal strike zone and as you prepare, rotate your shoulders, trunk, hips, and bend your knees. As you step forward to swing, simply uncoil the parts.

The energy is then transferred through your body, building at each link in the chain. It moves from your legs, through your hips, trunk, shoulder, arms, wrist, and finally to your racket. The end result is a faster, controlled swing that transfers speed onto the ball.

The speed at which you uncoil will correlate to more or less power. Experiment with uncoiling your body at varying speeds to develop a feel for adding power from your shots. Start with three power levels. For example.

> *It's like driving a car. Would you drive at a speed where you could have an accident every five minutes? Drive your car at a speed where you don't have a lot of accidents. Your role as a player is to play at a speed at which you don't miss. Find that speed.*
>
> **– Patrick Mouratoglou**
> **Former Coach of**
> **Serena Williams**

Power Level 1. This would be the pace that you would hit at when you're in a neutral rally where nobody has yet taken control of the point. For comparison purposes, to achieve this level of power, you'll uncoil your body at 50% of your maximum speed. This is the power level you'll use for most of your shots.

Power Level 2. When you have the opportunity to shift to offense and want to get the ball over the net quickly (e.g., passing shots, hitting aggressively to open the court, etc.), move to level 2. Your technique remains the same. What changes will be the speed at which you uncoil your body. Again, for comparison purposes, let's say you'll uncoil at 75% of your maximum speed.

Power Level 3. You're in trouble. Your opponent may have you scrambling, or you're poorly positioned for your next shot. Whatever the reason, you're on defense and need time. In this situation, your power level should come down, and you'll do that by swinging at about 35% of your max.

Two final things to keep in mind. First, uncoiling speeds will vary from player to player. Fifty percent of your maximum speed may be faster than fifty percent of mine. It doesn't matter. The idea is for you to be able to develop a feel for the three speeds as they relate to you.

Second, and I can't stress this enough, regardless of your uncoiling speed, your technique must remain consistent. When trying to hit harder, many players will add elbow, wrist, or body movements to their swing. Or, when trying to take pace off the ball, will shorten their swing and push the ball. Both can lead to less control. Your technique should remain the same regardless of how much or little power you're trying to generate.

When to Add Power

When players think of the power shots in tennis, most immediately go to the serve. Every day, recreational players toss the ball on their first serve and swing as hard as they can. They feel that if their big serve goes in, it will be so overwhelming that their opponents won't be able to return it. The truth is their big serves rarely go in. Hard, flat serves have very little margin for error. Plus, even when they do go in, they're really not that "big." A recent study showed that the average 4.0-level man serves at approximately 75 m.p.h. And those were the serves that went in the box, not the ones that hit the back fence.

Forget the big serve. A medium pace, well placed first serve that you can get in 75% of the time will cause your opponent far more problems than the occasional (not so) big serve.

Here are a few of the most common situations where you might want to add a bit of power to your groundstrokes:

- When you have a mid-court ball in your ideal strike zone.
- When hitting a passing shot.
- When returning a weak second serve.

Four times not to add power to your shot.

- If you're more than four feet behind the baseline.
- If you're more than four feet outside of the court.
- If the ball is out of your ideal strike zone.
- If the ball is inside the service line and below the height of the net.

In all of these situations, you're out of position, either relative to the court or the ball, so simply play the ball back safely to avoid making an error.

Power can definitely be a weapon in your game. However, it should never be achieved at the expense of control and consistency. Continue to work on your strokes and overall consistency. As your timing and technique improve, your shots will become significantly more powerful.

Chapter 13
How to Handle Tennis Emergencies

Tennis is frequently called a game of emergencies and the description is accurate.

During your matches, you'll frequently find yourself off balance, unable to prepare your racket quickly enough or create the proper amount of space between you and the ball. How you respond to these emergencies will usually determine whether you walk off the court in first or second place.

The first key to dealing with emergency situations is to accept that you're in one. If you're not balanced and it's time to hit the ball, you're in an emergency situation. Whether your preparation was sloppy, your opponent hit a great shot, or you got a bad bounce makes no difference. At that moment, you have to find a way to get the ball back over the net to stay in the point.

One of the things that separate players at the 3.5-level from those above is their response to tennis emergencies. The lower-rated player panics or becomes stubborn, and attempts to blast his way out of trouble. More often than not, this approach ends with a reckless, unnecessary error. The stronger player recognizes—and accepts—that they're in trouble. They get the ball back in play and force their opponent to hit another shot.

> *Rarely will you be in total control of what's happening on the court. In fact, if you are, you need to play against stronger players.*
>
> *– Peter Burwash*
> **Founder of PBI International**

Here are four of the most common emergency situations and some strategies for survival.

1. You're Pulled Way Off the Court

When your opponent moves you off the court, you have two immediate problems: you have to return the ball over the net as well as buy yourself time to get back into position.

Shorten your stroke, open your racket face (strings toward the sky), and hit a deep lob cross court. Lobbing will ensure that you clear the net, always your first obstacle. Plus, lobs travel through the air at a slower speed than a drive. That, combined with hitting crosscourt (a longer distance) will give you time to recover.

2. Your Opponent Attacks the Net

He's hit a strong approach shot and is charging the net. You have little time to prepare and zero chance of contacting the ball in your ideal strike zone. What do you do? Lob!

Get the ball over the net, push him back, and make him hit the most physically demanding shot in the game—the overhead. If you can lob over his backhand side, even better.

Some teaching pros advocate hitting a topspin lob. I don't. The topspin lob requires a tremendous amount of precision to hit properly and, when under pressure, most players simply can't execute it well. Instead, open your strings and hit up from underneath the ball. As you complete your swing, make sure your hand and racket head finish above your head. This will help you hit lobs with both height and depth.

3. Your Opponent Is Overpowering You

When playing a power player, it can seem like almost every shot you hit is an emergency. Don't make the mistake of trying to hit bigger than the big hitter. Slow your shots down and focus on hitting deep in the court. Approximately 50% of a player's power comes from his opponent's shot. If you give a big hitter little pace, he'll be forced to generate his own power. Big hitters don't like this. When forced to provide the power, they'll often overswing, lose control, and commit an error.

To take pace off your opponent's shots, shorten your backswing and hit with slice. The spin will slow the ball down and keep it low, making it difficult for your opponent to take a big swing and still maintain control of their shot.

Finally, when the big hitter has you scrambling, do not change the direction of the ball. If they hit cross-court, return his shot crosscourt. When under pressure, changing direction is extremely difficult.

4. Defending Against a Good Lob

You've attacked the net because your pro told you that you should, only to have your opponent hit a lob over your head. Now what?

Ideally, hit the ball before it bounces as it will allow you to maintain control of the net. If you can move back quickly, and balance yourself behind the ball, hit an aggressive overhead.

If you're struggling to get back, feel off-balance, or are forced to hit the ball from your backhand side, simply turn the shot into a high volley. Take the ball out of the air and use a short motion as if you were giving your opponent a high five. Bunt the ball back deep, maintain control of the net, and begin to anticipate the next shot.

An exception to this would be if you're playing outdoors and your opponent hits a high, defensive lob into the stratosphere. The higher the lob, the faster it will fall, making it more difficult for you to time. Let it bounce. The moonball lob will still bounce up high enough for you to hit an overhead.

Also, if you're looking into the sun, letting the ball bounce gives you more time to prepare. Be sure to use your non-racket hand to shield your eyes from the sun.

Worst-Case Scenario

There will be times when your opponent's lob is just too deep for you to hit out of the air. When this happens, sprint back as quickly as you can, trying to get behind the ball. Be sure not to run directly at the ball; circle around it instead.

As you're moving back, take a quick look at your opponent. If he's not moving forward to the net, return the ball deep down the center of the court.

More likely, when he sees you scrambling, he'll move in for the kill. Now, you'll have to come up with something other than just putting the ball back over the net. Throw up a high, deep, lob and make him deal with a difficult overhead.

When faced with your next tennis emergency, don't take the coward's way out and go for the impressive looking, low-percentage shot. Sure, sometimes you might pull one off. However, "sometimes" doesn't win matches at the higher levels of the game. I guarantee you that in the long run, you will win more points by playing smarter rather than going for broke.

Chapter 14
Avoid These Two Major Mistakes

I'd like to end this section by briefly talking about two aspects of hitting the ball that many recreational players pay little, if any, attention to. I'm talking about developing a strong serve and becoming comfortable using the continental grip. If you ignore both your game will ultimately plateau. I guarantee it.

The Serve

As you approach the 3.5 level, you'll need to upgrade your serve from simply being a way to start the point to becoming an offensive weapon. The first step toward this is to develop a reliable toss.

The truth is most 2.5 to 4.0 players struggle with their toss. They throw the ball in the air, search to find it, and then frantically adjust their swing to hit their serve. It should be the opposite. You should adjust your toss to the path of your swing. To check your toss, try this simple test.

1. Take your racket and go through your service motion.
2. Stop your arm in front of your body, at your point of contact.
3. Slowly drop your arm until your racket head touches the court in front of you. This will show you roughly where your toss should be. Place a hand towel on that spot.
4. Go through the motion again, this time tossing the ball and letting it drop to the court. Do this ten times and see how many tosses land on the towel. Anything less than eight means your toss needs work.

Here are two quick tips to help groove your toss:

1. Imagine balancing a glass of water in the palm of your hand as you release the ball. This will help you place the ball out in front of your body. I often have my students do this with an actual paper cup filled with water. It works wonders.
2. Try to toss the ball in the air without it spinning. This will help to cut down on any wrist flick or finger roll that can throw your toss off its course.

If you're struggling to control your toss using your full-service motion, start with your racket in the back-scratch position. Then you can focus solely on your tossing arm.

Remember, successful strokes are a function of positioning (spacing), and the positioning aspect of your serve is the toss. If every time you toss the ball, it's an adventure to find it, you'll never have a strong serve. However, once you gain control over your toss, you can begin to focus on making your serve a true weapon. This means being able to do two things:

1. Get a high percentage (over 70%) of first serves in play.
2. Put your opponent off-balance.

To do both, focus on spin and placement. Learn to hit both slice and topspin serves. These are best hit with a continental grip, which we'll get into in a moment. Becoming comfortable with this grip, and proficient with both spin serves, will immediately take your serve to the next level.

Once you've developed both spin serves, set up targets in the service box to work on placement. Place a target in each corner of the box and the third in the middle. Serve, aiming for each of the targets, and be sure to practice from both service boxes.

Once you're able to hit a serve with topspin and slice to all three targets from three different spots along the baseline (you should vary your position when serving), you'll have eighteen different serving options. Then, if you can throw in the occasional flat serve to all three spots, from all three areas of the baseline, you'll have 27 different serves at your disposal. That's the definition of a strong serve, and there's no excuse not to have one.

The Continental Grip

Master Teaching Professional Jorge Capestany says that the continental grip is "a non-negotiable technique. If a player doesn't invest in this grip, they'll miss out on a multitude of shots." I couldn't agree more.

Here are some of the shots that can be in your arsenal when you become proficient with the continental grip:

Aggressive serve

Slice groundstrokes

Under-spin approach shot

Volley

Drop volley

Defensive lob

Chip passing shot

Approach volley

Chip return

Drop shot

Lob volley

Overhead smash

When you begin to practice with the continental grip, you'll likely have little (if any) control over the ball, and your wrist might even feel as if it's going to snap. I can assure you that your wrist is not going to snap and eventually you'll learn to control the ball.

The reason the grip is initially uncomfortable is that you're holding the racket in a totally foreign way that forces you to recruit different muscles. The only way to overcome this is to hit balls—lots of them. I believe it takes between 1,000–2,000 strikes of the ball to begin to become proficient with a new grip or technique. If you're serious about improving, you'll put in the time.

There is no better way to become comfortable with the continental grip than to play mini tennis. Because of the slower pace and the much-smaller court area, you'll be able to develop a feel for how your racket face should be positioned at contact to direct the ball. Mini tennis emphasizes control, so

> *You must learn to become comfortable being uncomfortable.*
>
> *– Vic Braden*

practice hitting with slice. As you do, you'll be laying the foundation for a wide variety of shots.

High-level tennis players have variety in their games. The continental grip is the first, and perhaps most important, step toward giving you this variety. There is no debate: To be a complete player, you must become comfortable with the continental grip.

The Truth About Mini Tennis

At the recreational level, mini tennis has, unfortunately, become a casual activity that players do under the guise of warming up. They stand virtually still on the service line, sloppily pushing balls back and forth while chatting with their friends. It's a complete waste of time!

The truth is with the proper approach, mini tennis is an amazing training tool that will improve your game in many ways. Here are a few.

- **It's a great warm-up.** As you hit on the shorter court with active footwork, your heart will start pumping. You'll warm up your muscles and your eyes and begin to get a feel for hitting the ball.
- **It helps you to focus.** As you hit balls into the service box right from the start, you become locked into hitting to a target. It will then become much easier to back up and expand to the entire court.
- **Mini tennis helps you practice hitting with spin.** Playing on the short court, you'll be forced to slow your strokes down. This will help you focus on your technique for both slice and topspin.
- **Mini tennis will improve your movement.** You can practice your split step, shuffle steps, crossover steps, and recovery steps.
- **It can be an amazing workout.** The next time you and your practice partner take the court, play a few points of mini tennis, using both service boxes. You'll see what I mean.

Play mini tennis regularly with intent and energy. You'll be amazed how quickly your footwork, focus, and overall control improve.

Part 3
The Truth About Strategy

Accepting that tennis is a game of errors is your first step toward understanding strategy. From there, your approach should revolve around three questions:

1. What shots can I hit that will minimize the chances of me making an error?
2. What shots can I hit that will maximize the chances of my opponent committing an error?
3. What strategies will give me (or my team) the greatest chance of winning?

The answer to all these questions is high-percentage.

Well-executed, high-percentage tennis wins at every level of the game. In this section of the book, I'll go over high-percentage shots and strategies for doubles (the game most play) and singles.

Keep in mind that high percentage will change as your skills improve. For a player at the 4.5 level, hitting an aggressive overhead while standing midway between the service and baseline is likely a high-percentage shot. However, in that same situation for a 3.0-level player whose overhead hasn't yet developed, blocking the ball back deep in the court would be the high-percentage play.

For a 4.0 player with a strong serve and reliable volleys, serving and volleying is a high-percentage strategy. However, players who haven't yet developed their serve or volley, should serve and stay back as that will likely give them their highest-percentage chance for success.

Before we get into specifics, there are two strategic skills you must commit to developing.

Chapter 15
Patience

When players of equal ability face each other, the one who's more patient will win virtually every time. How do you develop patience? Cooperative drills where the goal is not to win a point but rather to keep the ball in play, to a certain area of the court, for a designated number of times. In other words, consistency drills.

When I was learning the game, my lessons consisted almost exclusively of consistency drills. I would walk onto the court, warm up, and my coach would say, "Let's start off with 25 crosscourt forehands beyond the service line."

I would stand in one corner, my coach in the opposite, and we would begin to rally. Back and forth, back and forth, until we hit 25 shots in a row beyond the service line. He never missed, I frequently did. If I accomplished the goal, we moved on to another consistency drill. If not, we kept trying until I did— even if it took the entire hour.

Did I find these drills boring? Absolutely. Did I complain? All the time. Thankfully, my coach ignored my whining and pressed on with the drills. As my consistency improved, my mind became calmer and my strokes smoother. I also complained a lot less.

Looking back, I realized that when I whined about the drills being too boring, I was really saying was that they were too hard. I didn't like the drills because I couldn't do them.

The skills I gained through these drills developed my mental endurance which in turn made me a more patient player. How did this show up in my matches? You got it—fewer unforced errors and more wins.

Aside from grooving the mechanics of my strokes, knowing that I could keep the ball in play gave me a tremendous amount of confidence during matches. It gave me the confidence to be patient and therein lies the key to strategy.

Consistency gives you the confidence to be patient

When you're confident in your ability to keep the ball in play, you've trained your mind to be patient. Players without this confidence can't properly develop points. After two to three shots, they become uncomfortable knowing they don't have the consistency to stay in an extended rally. They panic, go for a low-percentage shot, and hand their opponent the point with an unnecessary error.

> *Consistency is a mental weapon.*
>
> **– Nick Bollettieri**

Patience reduces errors, and the player who makes fewer errors will almost always win the match. Bottom line: become a more consistent player and you'll win more matches.

An online search will give you plenty of consistency drills that you can take to the court. Here are a few to get you started. They begin very basically and become more difficult as you move down the list. During all of the drills, be sure to keep your feet active, take strong split steps, and return to your ready position after each shot. Otherwise, you're wasting your time.

No matter how good you think you may be, start with the first drill. You might be surprised.

1. Stand on one service line with your practice partner on the other side of the net on his service line. Rally back and forth with short, controlled strokes, keeping the ball inside the service line. You should be able to consistently hit 25 in a row before moving on to the next drill.
2. Still on the service line, move diagonally across from each other and hit crosscourt forehands in the same manner. Short, controlled swings with every ball going crosscourt and landing inside the service line. Once you get 25 on a consistent basis, move on to drill number three.
3. Same drill, except now hit crosscourt backhands inside the service line. Hit 25 and then move on.
4. Stand directly across from your partner, you on the deuce side service box, your partner on his ad side. You hit forehands down the line, and

your partner returns with his backhand down the line. Again, with all shots landing inside the service line. When you hit 25 in a row, move on.

5. Switch sides and do the same drill. This time you are hitting backhands down the line, and your partner is hitting forehands down the line, 25 times.

Once you can consistently do these five drills, move back to the baseline and go through the sequence again. Rally using the entire court, then cross-court one way, then the other. Finally, go down the line on one side and then finish down the other.

When you can consistently complete all of these "consistency" drills, you'll be well on your way to becoming a more solid and strategic player.

Chapter 16
Awareness

One of my favorite teaching techniques is to ask questions. For example, after a missed shot, I might ask a player:

- "What were you trying to do with that shot?"
- "If that shot went in, how did you expect the point to progress?"
- "Before you hit that shot, where was your opponent positioned on the court?"

> *Most recreational players are brain-dead on the tennis court. They go out and run around with no plan, no thought, no nothing. They give it as much study and consideration as jumping rope. And that's why they can be had.*
>
> **– Brad Gilbert**
> **Professional coach and author of**
> ***Winning Ugly.***

Far too often, the response is a shrug of the shoulders followed by an embarrassed "I don't know." Well, if you don't know what you were trying to do or what was going to happen next, or even where your opponent was standing when you selected your shot, how can you expect to be successful? You can't!

Many players go through their matches totally unaware of what's happening on the court. They make poor strategic decisions, commit unnecessary errors, and end up losing matches they should win.

To begin to understand, and implement, any type of strategy, you must become aware of what's happening around you.

Situational awareness on the tennis court falls into three categories:

1. Ball awareness
2. Court awareness
3. Opponent awareness

Ball Awareness

This means becoming aware of the position of the ball relative to your body. In Chapter 8, I went through the various strike zones. As a reminder:

Strike zone #1: below your knees
Strike zone #2: from your knees to chest
Strike zone #3: above your chest

Most players prefer to hit their shots from zone 2. With that in mind, everything you do, from a preparation perspective, is with the goal of being able to hit your shot in zone 2. In a perfect world, all of your shots are hit from zone 2.

However, as I said, tennis is a game of emergencies, and often you'll have to hit a shot from an uncomfortable strike zone. Recognizing this is "ball awareness."

I can't tell you how often I see a player with the ball up around their ears or down by their ankles, try to make last-second adjustments and contortions in an attempt to blast their way out of trouble. These players suffer from a serious lack of "ball awareness", or just stubbornness.

When the time comes to swing your racket, you're either well-positioned or you're not. If you're poorly positioned, it doesn't matter why. You can work on that in a future practice session. At that moment, your only goal is to keep the ball in play.

The next time you practice, make a mental note of which zone each ball is in as you prepare to swing your racket. If it's in zone 2, then you can likely hit an aggressive shot. If it's not, accept it, play the ball back safely, and move on to the next ball.

Court Awareness

Court awareness means being aware of where you're standing on the court as you prepare to hit your shots. As with strike zones, there are varying thoughts among teaching pros as to how many areas of the court there should be. I'm a fan of the traffic light system. See below.

- **Red: behind the baseline**

When you're in red, you're likely in a neutral or defensive rally. Do not try to attack. The deeper you are on the court, the longer it will take for the ball to reach your opponent, giving him more time to prepare. Hit your shots deep and crosscourt. Your goal is to keep your opponent in their red area.

- **Yellow: between the baseline and service line**

Yellow is a transitional area. Do not try to end the point! Instead, proceed with caution. Begin to dictate play with your shots. If you're playing doubles, move to the net. If you're playing singles, move the ball around the court to force a short ball. When that short ball (around the service line) comes, hit it aggressively and move forward to green.

- **Green: inside the service line**

When you advance to green, keep the pressure on by hitting deep, anticipate lobs and passing shots, and look for an opportunity to end the point.

You can practice your court awareness in the same way you worked on ball awareness. As you rally with your practice partner, become aware of which color you're standing in as you prepare to hit each shot. Say "red, yellow, or green" to yourself.

Combining "ball awareness" with "court awareness" will go a long way toward helping you make smarter decisions. If you're an aware player, you'll recognize that, when you're six feet behind the baseline (red) and the ball is three feet above your head (strike zone 3), trying to hit an aggressive shot is a bad idea.

Conversely, when you find yourself in yellow (between the baseline and service line), and you've positioned yourself so that you can hit the ball in strike zone 2 (knees to chest), you'll know you can play an aggressive shot.

Opponent Awareness

Often players come to me after their matches and tell me everything their opponents did to beat them.

"They kept hitting down our alleys."
"When we came to the net, they lobbed over our heads every time."
"They put every volley away."

While these are all good observations and demonstrate a level of awareness, I want my players to take it to the next level and understand the role they played in allowing their opponents to do these things. For example:

If your opponents are	You're likely
Dominating at the net	Hitting short shots that are allowing them to come in.
Angling away their volleys	Giving them volleys in their comfortable strike zones.
Beating you down the alley	Not following the ball and shifting laterally to cover your alley.
Ripping their returns of serve	Hitting weak serves to their stronger side.

Simply complaining that your opponents did this or that is an easy cop-out. It's as if you're absolving yourself of any responsibility. The truth is your opponents can only do (or not do) what you allow. If you consistently feed them balls in comfortable strike zones, and areas of the court where they can be aggressive, you're going to struggle.

Once you accept this, you can then begin to employ tactics designed to break them down.

For example:

If you	Your opponents will be forced to
Hit high and deep	Hit their shots backing up and off-balance. This will often force a weak return or error.
Hit short and low	Scramble forward and pop the ball up. This is particularly effective when playing doubles.
Take the pace off your shots	Generate their own pace. Many players struggle with this and over-hit.
Attack the net	Hit difficult, high-pressure shots every time because you're in a position to end the point. This pressure will often force them into panic errors.

Once you develop patience and the three levels of awareness, you'll be much better able to use strategy to win your matches. Now, let's get into more specific strategies.

Chapter 17
How to Win the Warm-Up

Have you ever been on the court with a player who, during the warm-up phase, played as if it were the third-set tiebreaker?

While you're hitting medium-paced balls down the center of the court to find your rhythm and allow your opponent to do the same, he's blasting every second ball to a corner. He comes to the net to volley, and you feed him medium-speed, chest-high balls, as you should. Yet, when you come forward, he drills the ball at your naval or even at your feet.

Out of ignorance, arrogance, or selfishness, these players are trying to "win" the warm-up. Some may believe this is an intimidation tactic designed to set an aggressive tone and gain the upper hand at the start of the match. Whether or not that's the motive, I feel it's obnoxious and extremely poor tennis etiquette.

That said, "winning" the warm-up is an important element of match play, but in a much different way. The player who truly "wins"—or rather, benefits more from—the warmup is the one who, during this brief period of time, has gathered the most useful information about his opponent.

Many players believe that the main purpose of the warm-up is to groove their strokes and get their body moving. The truth is if you're a serious competitive player, you've stepped onto the court already warmed up.

You've hit balls with a friend or against a wall for 20–30 minutes to get all of your strokes grooved, and you've done some dynamic stretching to get your body moving freely. By the time you step on the court, you should be ready to play the first point.

You'll 'win' the warm-up—and have a big head start against your opponent—if, during those 10 minutes, you do an analysis of his game. That analysis will help you formulate smart tactics for the match.

The warming-up/sizing-up period begins the moment you and your opponent step onto the court. Start by looking at his physique. Is he tall? Is he short? Is he very thin? Is he overweight?

If your opponent is tall, make a mental note to hit a lot of low balls to make him bend. If he's short, then high balls during baseline rallies and lobs, when he comes to the net, will be effective.

If he's carrying a few extra pounds, moving him around the court and extending rallies could wear him down. And, if he's exceedingly thin, he might not be particularly strong. Maybe you can overpower him.

As you begin to hit back and forth, pay particular attention to these 10 things.

1. **Is he right or left-handed?** Surprisingly, some players don't notice this vital difference until they're told after the match. Approximately 85% of the players you'll ever face will be right-handed, so when you come up against a lefty, you'll need to keep a few things in mind.

   - His serves will spin the opposite way to what you're used to against right-handed players.

   - When serving to the ad court, most lefties possess a strong slice serve out wide. It's extremely effective against righties because it pulls them off the court and is to their backhand. To deal with this, position yourself an additional step or two to the left. When they serve, move forward to cut the ball off and take it on the rise. If the serve lands in the center of the box and has little power or spin, you might be able to run around your backhand and hit an aggressive forehand.

   - When you're receiving serve in the deuce court, look for a lot of serves down the T and position yourself accordingly. Move a little closer to the T, forcing him to serve to your forehand. Serving out wide in this court is difficult for most lefties.

   - When you're serving from the deuce court, slice your serve out wide to his backhand. This can often force a weak return, which you can then move forward and attack.

2. **Does he prefer to hit his forehand or backhand**? Feed a ball right at his body and see which stroke he chooses to hit. Do it three times. If

he chooses the same shot each time, you can be pretty certain that's his stronger, more confident side.

This is great information to have as you move through the match. Once you determine which side he prefers, hit a lot of balls to the other. You'll gain a sense of whether this side is a major weakness.

3. **What grips does he use?** Every grip has advantages and disadvantages. For example, if he uses a semi-western or western grip, he'll have a tough time with low balls, so slice a lot of your shots. If he uses a continental grip for groundstrokes, high-bouncing balls will give him fits. Also, he'll have an extremely difficult time hitting topspin groundstrokes.

4. **Does he hit a one-handed or two-handed backhand?** If he has a two-hander, he'll typically generate more power and topspin, but wide balls will give him trouble as will low shots and balls hit above his head. If he has a one-handed backhand, he may have trouble generating topspin and power and will also struggle with balls hit shoulder height or above.

5. **Does he move well and hustle after every ball?** Hit him a variety of shots: high, low, soft, hard, slice, and topspin. See how he reacts to each. "Accidently" hit a ball far away from him and see what he does. If he runs after a ball in the corner, he's likely a mover who's willing to chase down a lot of balls. If he lets some balls bounce twice, or moves causally to them, perhaps his movement is a weakness that can be exploited. Every now and then, add some power to your ball and see whether his technique and timing hold up.

6. **Does he read the ball well and react quickly?** Hit a few balls to the service line and see what happens. Does he quickly move forward or is he a little late recognizing the short ball and forced to sprint and lunge to reach it. Many singles players are extremely quick and agile moving side to side (because they primarily hit groundstrokes) yet move slowly and awkwardly when they're forced to move forward (because they seldom come to the net.)

7. **How is his net game?** When, or if, he comes to the net to volley, is another information-gathering opportunity. I say "if" because I've

actually seen players take no volleys or overheads during the warm-up. If he does come to the net, take note of where he positions himself. Some players will stand a foot or two from the net, while others may hit most of their volleys from the service line. Both extreme positions may indicate that they're not comfortable being at the net. Hit balls to both his forehand and backhand sides to determine which volley appears stronger. Hit a few balls at his chest and at his feet to see how well (or poorly) he reacts.

When he hits overheads, pay attention to how smoothly and quickly he moves back for the ball. Is he able to hit the overhead back to you (as is protocol), or does he seem to lack control? If he doesn't ask for overheads, it likely means it's a weakness. That's valuable information for your memory bank. Also, pay attention to your opponent when you come to the net. Is he able to control the ball back to you, or does he seem to struggle? Can he feed you consistent lobs?

8. **How does his serve look?** As he takes serves, pay attention to where the ball bounces. Does he serve to various areas of the service box or do all of his serves land on the same spot? Notice where he tosses the ball and then where the serve lands. Often, a player will tell you where he's going to serve by the placement of his toss.

9. **Take a close look at his body language:** Does he seem relaxed or uptight? Does he look excited about the match? Does he get angry with himself over missed shots? Paying attention to all of these clues—what poker players would call tells—will give you a sense of his temperament.

10. **Who is the stronger player on their doubles team?** If you're warming up for a doubles match, you and your partner should each pick a player on the opposing team and take note of all of the above. Also, try to determine which player appears to be the leader. Notice who initiates the conversations between the team. When you spin the racket, pay attention to which player calls "up or down" and makes the decision whether to serve or receive. That player may very well be the leader. The leader is often the stronger player and determining that as early as possible can give your team a big advantage.

These are just a few examples of things you can look for during the warm-up. Don't drive yourself crazy trying to analyze everything. If you can come away from the warm-up with one or two pieces of helpful information, you'll likely have "won" the warm-up.

Finally, while you're checking out your opponent, you can be certain they're doing the same. From the moment you step onto the court, present yourself as a strong, confident opponent. Stand tall, be alert, and project energy.

As you move through the warm-up, be on your toes, take strong split steps, keep the ball in play, and run after everything. Let your opponent see that you're a solid, composed player who is willing to chase down everything. That will send a very distinct message that he's going to be in for a tough battle.

> *The warm-up is not the time to practice your strokes. If you don't have the strokes when you arrive for the match, a 10-minute warmup won't improve them. The warm-up should be a period of observation of your opponent, not a time to get your game together. Don't focus your attention on yourself, but rather on your opponent.*
>
> **– Peter Burwash.**

Chapter 18
Never Serve First

Whether you're playing singles or doubles, at the 3.0 level, the 5.0 level, or somewhere in between, if you win the spin of the racket, make your opponent serve first.

The truth is most recreational players serve at a level or two below the rest of their games. They'll spend hours working on their groundstrokes and volleys and playing practice matches, but rarely will they take a basket of balls and work on their serve.

Here are a few more reasons to hand the balls to your opponent at the start of the match.

1. **He won't be properly warmed up.** Even if your opponent has a phenomenal serve, it will be at its weakest early in the match. He's probably not fully warmed up, won't yet have his timing, and may be a little nervous. His serve will likely improve as the match moves along, so catch him early.

> *The perceived advantage of serving first may apply in men's professional tennis, but it really doesn't anywhere else.*
>
> **– Brad Gilbert**

2. **You'll get into his head.** By letting your opponent serve first, you're basically telling him that his serve doesn't scare you.

3. **You can gain the upper hand.** If you break your opponent's serve, he'll suffer a letdown, having lost his serve to start the match. Plus, if you win your service game, he'll be down 0-2 with even more pressure to win his next service game.

4. **You'll be better prepared when it's your turn to serve.** Letting your opponent serve first creates a pressure-free game for you. If you lose

the game, it's no big deal—he's supposed to win his serve. When it's your turn to serve, you'll have had a bit more time to find your rhythm, get used to the speed of the court, and settle into the match.

Chapter 19
High-Percentage Doubles

Playing high-percentage doubles encompasses two things: positioning and shot selection. Which of the various formations will give your team the highest-percentage chance of winning the point? Then, from that formation, what are the highest-percentage shots to execute?

Positioning

At the 4.0 level and above, the team that controls the net wins the point 85% of the time. Here are three reasons why:

1. For most players, volleys are technically easier to hit than groundstrokes. Groundstrokes require more preparation, longer swings, and intense movement and timing. For the most part, volleys only demand that from the ready position you turn your shoulders move one or two steps, and then push your racket forward with minimal follow-through. If two players of equal ability get into a groundstroke/volley exchange, the baseliner will usually miss first.

1. A primary goal in doubles is to force your opponents to hit the ball up so you can then aggressively hit it back down. This means that (at the appropriate time) you can end the point either by driving a volley at your opponent's feet or hitting down the middle. You can't drive "down" from the baseline, only at the net.

> *Controlling the net in doubles isn't that important…only the good teams do it.*
>
> *– Ken DeHart*
> *USPTA and PTR Master Professional*

2. When your team controls the net, you take time away from your opponents. Your shots will appear to have more pace, and they must hit a quality shot every time they strike the ball. If they don't, you can end the point with one shot.

So, yes, the highest-percentage formation is two players at the net. However, to win, your team must move well and volley effectively. You must also be able to anticipate lobs and drives and hit solid overheads. These are skills that take time to develop. Your current level of play will dictate how successful this formation will be.

If you're a team at the 3.5 level or below, the one-up, one-back formation will likely give you the highest-percentage chance of winning matches. There's no shame in that. It is what it is—for now. However, if you want to move up to the 4.0 level, spend plenty of practice time developing your net skills.

Shot Selection

While angles and alleys may win points at the lower levels (where players don't cover the court properly) and senior tennis (where both the players and the ball move at a slow pace), in a fast-paced, doubles game, most points are won by hitting to three places:

1. Down the Middle

Hitting down the middle of the court always creates an element of confusion for the other team. It's always fun to watch your opponents give each other the "Where were you?" look after your shot goes untouched between them.

Plus, when you play down the center, your opponents must create their own angles—a difficult thing to do. Finally, if you hit down the center and don't hit the ball well, you'll probably still keep it in play. When you go for alleys and angles, only to miss your target, you'll likely lose the point with an error.

2. At Their Feet

Don't try to hit shots your opponents can't touch—hit shots they can't return.

Countless times I've seen a player miss an easy volley because he tried to keep it away from his opponent instead of hitting at his feet.

Forget about 'keeping it away' from your opponents—you'll make too many errors. Instead, work on placing the ball at awkward areas of their body (feet and hips) to force them to miss. If they do manage to get the ball back, it will likely be an easy sitter that you can attack.

> ### Hitting Your Opponents
>
> The truth is more often than not, when a player gets hit by a ball, it's his own fault. He's either not in the right position or not paying attention. Competitive doubles is a fast, aggressive game where quite often the most strategic shot is right at the opposing player. It's up to everyone on the court to remain focused and properly positioned. If you do accidentally hit someone, immediately make sure he's OK, and in the spirit of good sportsmanship, raise your hand as a sign of apology. Be sincere, but don't hesitate to go at them again.

3. Over Their Heads

The lob is the most powerful shot in tennis. By powerful, I don't mean pace. I mean impact on the point. Be it the low, offensive lob to push your opponents from the net or the high, deep defensive lob that gives you time to recover, every high-level team understands the benefits of an effective lob. It's a must-have shot.

People make fun of those players who like to throw up a lob every two or three shots, but they seem to forget that good lobbers have more trophies than any other person at the club.

– Vic Braden

When teams at the 4.0 level and above compete, they play long, strategic points with lots of lobs. These players have gotten over the ego boost of hitting that rare world-class/lucky shot and understand that the lob is one of their most effective weapons.

When your opponents take control of the net, and you're not confident you can drive a low shot, lob. Force them to move back and hit an overhead, the most physically demanding shot in the game.

Avoid Alley Obsession

Attempting to hit down your opponent's alley is one of the lowest-percentage shots in doubles. Here's why:

- The alley is just 54 inches wide, plus the net is higher at the ends than at the center. Stand at the baseline and drop and hit ten balls, aiming for the alley. You'll see how difficult executing the shot is.
- To hit the alley, you'll usually have to change the direction of the ball. Not an easy thing to do.
- If you don't hit the shot perfectly, you're giving your opponent two easy options to beat you: they can volley down the middle or drill it at your partner.

Three scenarios in which you should hit to the alley are if your opponent:

- Leaves it open.
- Volleys poorly
- Actively poaches

At the 4.0 level and above, the first two scenarios largely disappear. Experienced players cover their alley and volley well. Take a quick look and, if the player hasn't shifted to cover his alley, go for it. However, if he has, don't be stubborn, return the ball crosscourt, and continue the point.

In high-level doubles, the only time to target the alley is when the net player is actively poaching. Then, the occasional alley or body shot will help keep him honest.

To sum up: Control the net and win your points by hitting down the middle, at your opponent's feet, or over his head.

Chapter 20
Strategies Against Teams
with Different Styles of Play

Most doubles teams fall into one of three categories.

1. Net rushers
2. teams that play one up and one back
3. teams that play both players back

Here are some high-percentage strategies for each.

Net Rushers

When you're up against a hard-charging team, you're facing opponents that understand doubles. They've learned that, if they can gain control of the net, they'll likely win the point. As a result, they're looking for any opportunity to come forward. To beat this type of team:

- **Win the race to the net.** Net-rushing teams are often uncomfortable in the backcourt, so do all you can to beat them to the net. You and your partner should come in behind your serves and as soon as you can after your return of serve. If you lose the race to the net, resist the urge to try to hit clean winners or drill the ball through your opponents. While this may work with players who haven't yet developed their volley and movement skills, against an experienced team, your ship will sink fast. Instead, patiently mix up low balls to draw them closer to the net and high balls to push them back. Keep them moving and wait for an error or weak shot that you can move forward to attack.

- **Lob and then lob more.** After a few overheads, even the fittest players will start breathing heavily. Keep in mind that your goal with your lob is not to hit it over your opponent's heads. If you do, great, but experienced teams will likely anticipate your lob and start tracking back early. That's OK because if you can force them to hit overheads from behind their service lines, you've opened up a lot of court for your next shot.

When returning serve against an attacking team, a great tactic is to hit one down-the-line lob return and one hard return right at the net player during your first return game. Doing this will definitely give them something to think about.

Teams that Play One Up and One Back

Teams that play from this formation believe they're got the game figured out: one player covers the net and the other the backcourt. That's fine—as long as their opponents agree to play the same way.

The truth is the one-up-and-one-back formation is generally considered the worst of the various formations. When one player is up and the other back, there's a big hole down the center of the court. Plus, when your team takes control of the net, the single net player on the other team becomes a sitting duck.

The next time you find yourselves in a match against a team that plays one up and one back, you and your partner should:

- Both move to the net ASAP. This gives you two players against one at the net—a huge advantage.
- Hit to the baseliner player until you can get to the net. Once there, volley back to that same player until you get the shot—typically a high volley or easy overhead—that you can end the point with. When that ball comes, drive it between your opponents or at the feet of the opposing (closer) net player.
- Lob over the single net player and move forward, taking control of the net. After you lob, come in to just behind your service line. Your opponent, who's had to sprint across the court to get to your lob, will

almost certainly lob the ball back. Being farther back, you'll be well-positioned to handle his lob. Yes, you'll be standing in no-man's-land, but that's OK. The danger of being there is that your opponent will drive a ball down at your feet or angle it away from you.

Given they're scrambling across the court to cover your lob (which will bounce up over their shoulders), neither scenario is likely to happen.

Teams that Play Both Players Back

When a team positions both players at the baseline, it means they like to play defense and wait for you to self-destruct. Typically, they plant themselves behind the baseline, lob a lot, and wait for you to hand them the match. Here are a few tips to avoid falling into their trap.

- Get to the net and take control of the point.
- Anticipate lobs and drives and be prepared to return a lot of both.
- If you're forced to volley from below the net, slightly open your racket face and aim higher over the net to return the ball deep. If the volley is shoulder height, quickly move forward to end the point with a drop volley.
- If you're hitting an overhead from behind the service line, put the ball back in play and wait for something shorter. If you're inside the service line, look to end the point with a strong overhead.

Above all, be patient! Defensive teams thrive on their opponents losing their patience and making reckless errors. You and your partner must accept that, to beat a defensive team, you'll need to hit a lot of balls.

Chapter 21
High-Percentage Singles

During the first two or three games, simply hit the ball down the middle of the court. This will keep your ball away from the sidelines and traveling over the lowest part of the net. It will also allow you to settle into a comfortable rhythm, shake off any nerves and find out a key piece of information: Can your opponent keep the ball in play?

At the 3.0 level and below, this is likely the only strategy you'll need. Many players at these levels have a two to three shot attention span. After that, their mind wanders, and their patience evaporates. They go for a reckless, low-percentage winner and hand you the point.

As you move to the 3.5 level and above, consistency alone will likely not be enough. Then, you should shift to playing high-percentage singles. Here are a few strategies to keep in mind.

1. Again, Forget the Big Serve

Many players today adopt the blast and push approach to serving. They fire away on their first serve, thinking that if it goes in, they'll get an easy point as well as intimidate their opponent with their awesome power. They feel it's a no-brainer approach because, if it doesn't go in, they can always push in their second serve and still be in the point.

This may be effective at the 3.0 level and below where players don't have the skills to take advantage of a weak second serve. However, at the 4.0 level and above, a strong opponent will eat your "push" serve for lunch.

Unless you can consistently hit your first serve in the court at more than 100 m.p.h. (you can't and neither can I), going for the big serve is a waste of time and effort. Instead, view your serve as a tool to gain control of the point.

Strive to get 75% of your first serves in. Back off on the power and focus on spin and placement.

For placement, you have three primary targets: down the T, to the body and out wide. Of course, as the match progresses, you can adjust if you notice your opponent is significantly weaker returning on one side or the other.

2. Get Every Return of Serve Back in Play

Against a strong server on his first serve, think "react." Use his pace and block the serve back. Aim your returns five to seven feet above the net and down the middle of the court. If he serves and volleys, aim one to two feet over the net and block your return down at his feet.

If the first serve is missed, shift into attack mode. Many teaching pros tell their students to move forward a few steps so that they can jump all over the weaker second serve. I strongly disagree.

When players think about jumping all over a second serve, more often than not they wind up getting too close to the ball and their stroke collapses.

Attack doesn't mean you should try to end the point with one big shot. It means take control. Step into the ball, drive a deep crosscourt return and begin to dictate play.

Depending upon the quality of your opponent's second serve, you may be able to move forward and attack the net. If so, think of your return as an approach shot. Hit it straight ahead and move into the net. Another option is to attack with touch and occasionally hit a drop shot off his soft, short second serve.

3. Aim Higher Over the Net to Hit Deep

In a singles rally, the quality of your shot is largely determined by its depth. Strive to keep the ball within three feet of your opponent's baseline. To do this, aim five to ten feet over the net. Generally speaking, the lower your net clearance, the shorter your ball will land in the court. The pros masterfully use height to enhance both their groundstroke depth and consistency. Below are Rafael Nadal's, Roger Federer's and Djokovic's average net clearance with their forehands during a recent season.

Nadal: 90 inches

Federer: 70 inches

Djokovic: 63 inches

The net height in the middle is 3 feet (36 inches). Roger Federer (at 70 inches) is hitting at a height of nearly two nets and Nadal (at 90 inches) comes close to three.

4. Hit Your Groundstrokes Crosscourt

Eighty to ninety percent of your groundstrokes should be hit crosscourt. The ball will travel over the lowest part of the net, and the court is longer on the crosscourt diagonal. This means that you can hit the ball harder and farther and still keep it in play.

Also, by hitting crosscourt, you'll make your opponent run farther than if you hit down the line. The next time you practice, have one player hit all of his shots crosscourt while the other hits only down the line.

You'll soon see that the player hitting down the line is doing much more running. Not only does this illustrate the point, it's also a great consistency, speed, and conditioning drill.

As the point progresses, you're waiting for your opponent to make one of three mistakes:

> *I believe successful tennis is a game of consistency and taking advantage of the proper percentages.*
>
> **– Bjorn Borg**
> **Tennis Legend**

1. An impatient error that gives you the point.
2. A down-the-line shot that allows you to drive the ball crosscourt and run them off the court.
3. A short ball that allows you to move forward and attack.

In a baseline rally, position yourself diagonally across from where your opponent will be hitting their shot. From this position, you'll be able to efficiently move to cover your opponent's likely crosscourt return. The only exception occurs when you hit your shot right down the middle of the court. Then, recover to the center of the court.

5. Hit Your Approach Shots Straight Ahead

There's an old saying that "the point doesn't begin until someone hits a short ball." When that short ball comes, move forward and hit your approach shot straight ahead of where you strike the ball.

This will get the ball back to your opponent faster and also allow you to simply move forward to be in the proper position at the net.

Plus, by approaching straight ahead, you'll always be in your opponent's line of vision. As they move to hit their shot, seeing you directly in front of them will make them feel more pressured. On the other hand, if you hit crosscourt, he'll be looking at a wide-open court in front of him, or he'll be able to hit behind you as you sprint diagonally across the court to get to the net.

6. Take Control of the Net

Yes, even in this day of high-powered groundstrokes, the player who controls the net in singles controls the point. Look for every opportunity to move forward. However, keep in mind that, since you don't have a partner to help you at the net, you need to be more selective as to when you move forward. Be sure that the shot you've hit, or the shot you're about to hit, puts your opponent on the defensive before you move in.

Once you get to the net, remember that rarely will your first volley be the one that you can end the point with. Be prepared to hit at least two volleys. Play the first one back deep. After that, you can look for a volley to put away. Pick one that is above the net and that you can move forward to hit.

When you control the net, the pressure is on your opponent so don't force anything. If it takes two or three volleys and an overhead to win the point, so be it.

7. Be Patient

Be it a singles or doubles match with players of equal ability, it is the player (or team) who is more patient and willing to, as I like to say, suppress the stupidity that will usually come out on top.

Chapter 22
Strategies Against Players with Different Styles of Play

As your game improves, so will the level of your competition. You'll find yourself across the net from opponents that have varying styles of play. Most will fall into one of these four categories.

1. Big hitter
2. Human backboard
3. Net rusher
4. Junk ball artist

Here are some high-percentage strategies you can use against each.

The Big Hitter

Loves to use power to dictate play. He relies on his big groundstrokes to move you around the court and is not afraid to go for winners from the backcourt. He generally has a major weapon (usually his forehand) and eagerly uses it to end points. Because he's spent so much time developing his aggressive groundstrokes, the big hitter often volleys poorly, and as a result, does not like to come to the net. To handle the big hitter:

- **Extend the points.** The big hitter likes to end points quickly and is not used to—or comfortable with—his shots being returned. Commit to being a retriever and getting as many balls back in play as possible. Often, this will frustrate him into trying to hit even bigger, leading to errors.

- **Mix up the height, pace, and spin of your balls.** Keep the ball out of his preferred strike zone (usually knees to chest) where he can take aggressive swings. Mix in high-bouncing shots with low balls. Vary your spin and pace. The power player depends on rhythm. Disrupt it.

- **Hit short balls and drop shots to bring him forward.** Force him to come to the net, where he'll be less comfortable and effective. The key is to move him off the baseline—his happy place.

- **Weather the storm.** The big hitter tends to be a very up-and-down player. He'll hit his share of winners, but he'll also make a lot of errors. When he gets on a hot streak and is blowing you off the court, don't panic. Slow down the pace of the match. Get as many balls back in play as possible and wait for him to cool off. Eventually, he will.

The Human Backboard

Never misses, usually moves very well, and plays superb defense. He understands that tennis is a game of errors, knows the percentage shots, and seldom takes risks. He waits for you to lose your patience, go for too much, and hand him the match with errors. The next time you face a human backboard:

- **Be prepared for a long match.** Whether you like it or not, you're going to have to hit a lot of balls to win. It is what it is. Patiently keep the ball in play, move it around, and seize your first opportunity to go on the offensive.

- **Attack the net.** The human backboard loves to hang out in the backcourt and slow down the pace. He doesn't like to be rushed and doesn't want to be pressured into hitting more difficult shots. The moment you get a ball that floats or lands a little shorter in the court, move to the net.

- **Move them forward and backward.** The human backboard generally moves very well from side to side, but sometimes not so well forward and back. Probe and test him. Hit drop shots to pull him forward and then a deep lob to push him back. Try hitting behind him. This will be particularly effective on a clay court where footing is not as secure. These tactics can break his rhythm and force weak shots or errors.

- **Be prepared to deal with a lot of lobs.** The human backboard understands the power of the lob and how it frustrates opponents. To avoid getting into a never-ending lob fest, look for a lob that's a little shorter, move forward, and take it out of the air with a high volley or overhead.

The Net Rusher

Understands that the easiest place on the court to end the point is at the net. As a result, he moves forward as soon, and as often, as possible. To be successful against net rushers you need to:

- **Keep your shots deep in the court.** Try to keep all your groundstrokes—within three feet of the baseline. This will make it more difficult for him to move into a good net position. Remember, to hit deep, aim higher over the net.
- **Work on developing reliable passing shots and lobs.** These are the shots you'll need against the net rusher. Many players panic when they see their opponent charging toward them. If you can stay calm under pressure and execute good passing shots and lobs, you'll force him to hit challenging volleys and overheads. This will make him a little less confident each time he moves forward.
- **Beat him to the net.** Often, the player who loves the net hates the baseline. He's not confident in his ability to be consistent from the backcourt and his groundstrokes frequently collapse under pressure. Here you can use several tactics to beat him to the punch. You can follow your serve to the net. You can attack his second serve and you can sneak in behind deep groundstrokes and lobs. All will definitely take him out of his comfort zone.

The Junk Ball Artist

Thrives on ugly tennis and wins by frustrating his opponent. He hits softer balls, uses different spins, and waits for his opponent to fall apart. You must accept this and understand that you won't be able to play your normal game. When faced with one of these annoying players, be sure to:

- **Play closer to the baseline**. Junk ball players hit with less power so their shots will tend to land shorter in the court.

- **Pay close attention to his strokes.** Watch his racket to read what the ball is going to do once it gets to your side of the court. For example, if he swings from a low to high position, across his body (your left to your right), the ball will be hit with sidespin and move in the opposite direction (your right to your left) of the racket path when it bounces. If you pick up on this, you'll be able to position yourself properly.

- **When possible, come forward and hit the ball before it bounces.** This will eliminate having to deal with awkward bounces.

- **Keep your body low.** The junk ball player will hit balls with lots of slice which will keep his shots very low. To handle these, you'll need to be prepared to bend your knees more than usual and be sure to swing through the ball. Slow-moving balls that are hit with lots of spin tend to die on your racket. Don't push your shots. Instead, take a confident, long, and relaxed swing through the hitting zone.

Chapter 23
Winning Against Stronger and Weaker Players

There are going to be times when you step onto the court and your opponent is significantly stronger or weaker than you. You may know this going into the match from a scouting report or watching him play, or you figure it out early on. Both situations pose interesting challenges.

Facing a Much Stronger Opponent

The good news is that, when your opponent is significantly stronger, you can relax, have some fun and work on your game. There's no pressure because no one expects you to win.

With nothing to lose, some players feel they might as well throw caution to the wind and go for it. They launch one low-percentage shot after another in the hope that they'll catch fire and pull off an upset. Bad idea. You may briefly catch fire and come up with a few amazing shots, but more often than not, the flame will quickly burn out.

Instead, when facing a much stronger opponent, make them earn the win. Put as many balls back in play as possible and slow down the tempo of the match. Take your time between points and during changeovers—within the rules, of course.

If he hits much harder than you're used to, fight the urge to try to keep up with his power. Prepare faster by shortening your shoulder turn and speeding up your footwork. After a while, you'll adjust to his pace.

If he's a net rusher, focus on keeping your groundstrokes deep by aiming higher over the net. That depth will make it more difficult for him to come in. When he does get to the net, don't go for the low percentage passing shot that you'll likely miss. Make him hit the ball to beat you. Hit low balls and lots of lobs. If you can make him hit two or three overheads every time he comes to the net, you may very well wear him out

If he's a human backboard, make your way to the net and force him to hit his groundstrokes under pressure. You can also bring him forward. Most baseliners aren't comfortable hitting volleys and overheads.

The key is to show him that you're not going to roll over just because he's supposed to be better than you. If you can stay with him during the first few games or the first set, you may be able to crawl inside his head. He may start to tighten up. As the better player, he knows that he's supposed to win, and that presents a whole different type of pressure.

You're the Better Player

Being the higher-rated player (or team) can affect your game in In two ways: You might underestimate your opponent and relax too much, or you may feel the pressure of having to win and tighten up. In both situations, attitude is everything.

When you walk onto the court for a match you should win, push aside the feeling that the match is going to be easy. Overconfidence has led to many upsets. Remind yourself that your opponent is going to view the match as an opportunity. He's not supposed to win, so he'll be relaxed and likely play his best tennis. Play with the same point-by-point focus you would when playing an equal or stronger player and expect your opponent to start off strong.

When the top pros play a lower-ranked opponent, you'll frequently see the underdog stay with the favorite for the first six or seven games. They might even win the first set. After that, the weaker player either can't sustain the level of play, or the stronger player has figured out and exploited his opponent's weakness and pulls away.

If you find yourself playing an opponent who is one or more NTRP points below you, use the match to practice elements of your game that need work. Much weaker opponents will not present a serious threat to win the match. Even if they take a few games, you'll be able to firm up and finish the match on top.

Final thought. Just because you think you should win doesn't mean you will win. Across the world, underdogs pull upsets every day. Take the match seriously, remain focused, and if you truly are the better player that day, you'll prove it.

Chapter 24
Seizing the Momentum

Years ago, I was playing a tournament match and winning easily. I'd won the first set 6-1 and was up 5-2 in the second. Sixty minutes later, I walked off the court having lost the match 1-6, 7-5, 6-1. What happened? I had the momentum and then I lost it.

Momentum is that feeling that things are going well and, if you can keep it up, you'll likely win the match. How do you get it? Why do you lose it? And, once you lose it, how can you get it back?

Establishing Momentum

1. **After winning a point, pick up the pace.** Move more quickly than usual to begin the next point and play that point aggressively. Warren Pretorius, the founder of Tennis Analytics, says that Rafael Nadal takes three seconds less between points when he has won the previous point. Go for a slightly more aggressive serve or return. Put pressure on your opponent by attacking the net. Your goal is to make your opponent feel rushed and to win a few points in a row.

2. **Pick on your opponent's weaknesses.** If you notice, he struggles with overheads, draw him to the net and lob. If he doesn't like softer shots, take the pace off your balls. If his backhand is weak, hit everything to that side. By consistently picking on his weaker strokes, you'll draw errors, wound his confidence, and build your momentum.

3. **Keep him moving.** The more you can make your opponent scramble, the less confident he'll be executing his strokes. Plus, you'll begin to tire him out, which will lead to more errors for him and momentum for you.

4. **Don't take your foot off the gas.** One of the most common momentum busters is complacency. You win the first set and relax. Your opponent, fighting for his life, wins a few games. Your nerves then kick in, and you begin to play tentatively. Never forget that the match is not over until you shake hands at the net.

Lost Momentum

It can happen quickly. You miss a few balls, your opponent hits a lucky shot, he gives you a bad line call, and you've suddenly lost four games in a row. When you feel the match beginning to slip away, keep your cool. Slow down, take a deep breath, and try to understand why the momentum shift happened.

Did you lose your concentration, or did your opponent change his strategy? When he fought back and won a game or two, did you panic and move away from your game plan? Once you understand why you lost the momentum, you can begin to bring it back.

Regaining Momentum

Slow down! When the momentum moves against you, it's natural to shift into panic mode and speed up. Your mind starts to race, you begin to rush and try to end points quickly.

Your opponent, recognizing he now has the momentum, will want to speed things up and finish the match as quickly as possible. Do not let that happen. Take your time between points, games, and during changeovers. The pros, when they feel they're losing momentum, often choose that time to take a bathroom break.

Commit to playing consistent tennis. Momentum is often a function of consistency and consistency is a mindset. A huge part of that mindset is self-discipline. You must be disciplined in order to not let the peaks and valleys of a match affect you.

In my match described above, I had the momentum on my side and was serving at match point. I'd hit a strong serve, my opponent hit his return, and the ball hit the top of the net and plopped over to my side. Lucky net cord winner.

I got annoyed because I thought the match would soon be over. My opponent was energized because he survived match point. That's when the momentum shifted, and I ultimately lost the match I was so close to winning. How could that have happened?

It happened because my opponent, after hitting that lucky winner, got pumped up. His attitude and focus improved, and he began to play at a higher, more consistent level. I became negative. My patience ran low and my consistency and confidence disappeared. He stole the momentum, and ultimately the match, from me.

> *Momentum is facilitated by a great mindset.*
>
> **– Nick Saviano**
> **Owner, Saviano**
> **High Performance Academy**

Had I been more disciplined mentally, I would have been able to push aside my anger at my opponent's lucky shot, maintain my consistency and, most likely, the momentum I'd established.

Keep in mind that the scoring system in tennis makes it much easier for you to regain momentum than in many other sports. At the end of every set, you get to start over. The score goes back to 0-0. That clean slate can provide you with a great psychological lift and an opportunity to reset and reverse the momentum.

Chapter 25
How to Sabotage Your Opponent

Each year, the Tennis Congress (tenniscongress.org.) puts on amazing events designed to give recreational tennis players the opportunity to learn from some of the top coaches in the game. I strongly urge you to check them out.

At a 2016 event, USPTA Master Professional Jorge Capestany gave a great presentation called "Sabotage Tactics: How to Make Your Opponent Play Worse." Listening to Jorge's presentation gave me a serious moment of déjà vu.

Years ago, I was in the second set of a college match against a higher-ranked player named John. My groundstrokes were strong, my volleys crisp. I was moving well, and my first serve percentage was in the 80s. I was playing great yet found myself down a set and 0-3.

> *The key to beating any player is to take him out of his rhythm.*
>
> **– Martina Navratilova**
> **Tennis Legend**

During the changeover my coach, the legendary Norm Copeland, came over to me. The exchange went something like this:

Norm: *"What do you think?"*

Greg: *"I think I need to hit harder. Be more aggressive and go for more winners. I have to play better."*

Norm (never one to mince words): *"Greg, you can't play any better than this. If you want to win this match, you need to make John play worse."* Then, Norm walked over to the next court to coach one of my teammates.

Make John play worse? Since I had no idea what that meant, I walked back onto the court and deployed my original strategy: Hit harder, be more aggressive, and go for more winners. The match was over 15 minutes later.

When we fall behind, our natural reaction is to feel the need to raise our level of play to get back in the match. This is extremely difficult to do because we're most likely already playing at the highest level we have on that day. No one goes into a match thinking, "I'll start off playing at 70% of my best and then ramp it up if I need to." It just doesn't work that way.

The next time you find yourself struggling from behind, instead of trying to lift your game to meet your opponent's level of play, try bringing their level down to meet yours.

When your opponent has a big lead, he feels comfortable. He's hitting his shots from balanced positions and in his preferred strike zone. You need to take that comfort away. Here are three tactics that will do just that.

1. **Slice more balls.** When you slice well, your shots will stay lower. This will force your opponent to bend more—something most players don't like to do—and make it more difficult for him to hit aggressive, topspin returns. Here are two ideal strategies to deploy with slice:
   - **Change the rhythm of the rally.** In a topspin, baseline rally, returning balls coming at the same speed is relatively easy. If you throw in a sudden slice, it will act like a change-up from a pitcher in baseball and upset the rhythm of your opponent's movement as well as the timing of his strokes.
   - **Force a baseliner to come to net.** If your opponent loves to plant himself on the baseline and tee off on his groundstrokes—as so many players do today—bring him forward with a low, mid-court slice. This tactic will move him into an area of the court where he's going to be less comfortable. It will also force him to play the net, something baseliners tend to be uncomfortable doing.

Here are three quick tips to remember when hitting slice:

i. Change your grip quickly. You don't want to arrive at the ball and then rush to switch to a Continental grip.

ii. Prepare your racket approximately six inches above the ball and keep your racket face slightly open. This will allow you to brush under the ball as you swing forward and through your shot.

iii. Swing from high to low as your racket makes contact with the ball. When slicing, the shape of the swing is similar to a banana—the racket should be moving forward and slightly upward.

2. **Use the drop shot.** The drop shot is a fabulous sabotage technique that you frequently see used on the pro tour. It can work for you as well. Below are two high-percentage situations to use the drop shot to throw your opponent off his game.

   - **When your opponent is more comfortable at the baseline than the net.** In today's game, many players are better playing from the baseline. As a result, they tend to be most comfortable moving from side to side as opposed to forward and back. Hitting drop shots will not only surprise them, but it will also break their rhythm during the rally and force them to quickly scramble forward.

   - **As an approach shot.** Imagine this scenario: The last three times your opponent, he has hit you a short ball, you've moved in, hit a deep approach shot to his backhand corner, and rushed the net. Now he's hit another short ball. As you move forward to attack, what do you think he's going to expect? Another deep ball to his backhand corner, of course. As he instinctively backs up in anticipation, surprise him with a drop shot and follow it up to the net. Even if he can respond quickly enough to reach your drop shot, he now has to contend with you at the net. It's a smart tactic to throw opponents off balance.

When practicing your drop shot remember:

   - The drop shot is an exaggerated slice where you bring your racket from a high-to-low position. At contact, scoop under the ball. This adds backspin, which will slow the ball down and can even make it bounce backward if enough spin is applied. The feeling is similar to scooping ice cream out of a box.

- Two key elements of the drop shot are disguise and surprise, so you need to make your opponent think that you're going to hit your normal groundstroke. Approach the ball with your regular groundstroke preparation (racket high), but instead of driving through the ball, at the last second, scoop under it to hit the drop shot.

A word of caution: Never hit drop shots when you're moving backward or out of position. To use the drop shot effectively, you need to have your feet balanced and positioned firmly below you. Also, don't become addicted to it. If you hit it too often, you'll become predictable. If your opponent starts to anticipate your drop shots, he'll get to them quickly and attack your short ball.

3. **Hit moonballs.** Players who hit a lot of moonballs (very high lobs) during rallies are arguably the most frustrating to play against. When you hit a moonball, you'll accomplish several things.

   - You'll force him to back up far behind the baseline, giving you a positional advantage.
   - Because moonballs bounce so high, he'll be forced to hit his shot from above his shoulders—a very awkward position. As a result, he won't be able to strike the ball with much authority. This will drive power players crazy.
   - Your moonballs will slow down the pace of a match—something a player with a lead definitely does not want.

Here are two tips to keep in mind when working on your moonball.

- A moonball should travel very high over the net and land deep in your opponent's backcourt. The next time you and your practice partner take the court, place a string across the court, 3 feet inside each baseline. If you're playing on a clay court, you can draw this line on the court with the head of your racket. Rally back and forth with each of you trying to hit your moonball within this area.

- Moonballs can be hit with slice. However, topspin is much more effective as the ball will bounce higher and faster toward your opponent.

Players who can hit with slice, use drops shots, and moonballs are among the most frustrating opponents a player can face. It's no wonder they win a lot of matches.

Chapter 26
Tips to Win Tiebreakers

Whether it's to decide the winner of a set or the match, a tiebreaker presents a true tennis gut check. The mindset you bring to the tiebreaker and the way you handle tiebreaker pressure will determine how well (or poorly) you play the next seven to twenty points.

Before the first point, give yourself a quick attitude check.

1. **Are you excited to be in a tiebreaker?**
2. **Are you annoyed that the set will be decided by a tiebreaker?**
3. **Did you accept that the tiebreaker was inevitable?**

Each of these scenarios puts you in a different mindset. Being aware of your attitude, and knowing how to respond best to each scenario, will go a long way toward helping you play your best tennis over the next 10-15 minutes.

If you've made a great comeback and have the momentum going into the tiebreaker, you want to keep it going (see chapter 24).

If you're angry that you've given up a big lead, remind yourself it doesn't matter that you were up a set and 5-2. You're now totally even and have as much chance of winning the set or match as your opponent.

As I said earlier, that's one of the unique aspects of tennis' scoring system. You have many opportunities to reset, and that's exactly what you must do. Forget the past and focus on regaining the momentum.

If you were expecting a tiebreaker, now's the time to be sure your footwork and focus are at their best. As the previous twelve games have been close, the tiebreaker will likely be the same. One tactical mistake or careless shot from you or your opponent could make the difference between winning and losing.

Tiebreaker Pressure

The pressure of a tiebreaker has brought many a player's inner critic to a dangerous level:

"Oh God, a tiebreaker. I haven't won one of these in ten years."
"This is where my serve always falls apart."
"My arm feels like it weighs 100 pounds."
"I think I may throw up."

To play your best tennis, you must stop the flow of negativity and turn your inner voice into an ally. When bad thoughts bombard you, take a deep breath, give yourself a gentle slap on the thigh, and say to yourself, "No! I'm not going to do this." It sounds cliché, but it does work.

> *Smile when the critic comes knocking. Don't fight him. Laugh at him. You are in control and busy enjoying the competition.*
>
> *– Jeff Greenwald*

Replace the negativity with positive thoughts and visualizations. Rather than telling yourself how much you hate tiebreakers, say, "Seven more points and I win the set. Play percentage tennis, hustle after every ball, and refuse to miss." Close your eyes and envision yourself serving out wide, forcing a short return. See yourself moving forward and hitting into the open court. If you say—and see—it enough, you can make it happen.

Tiebreaker Scoring

Consider the following:

- To capture a set, you need to win by a margin of two games. To win a set through a tiebreaker, you need to win by a margin of only two points.
- Over the course of a set, you could lose seven out of ten points or even seven points in a row and still win the set. In a standard tiebreaker, if either scenario happens, you lose the set.

The message here is that each point in a tiebreaker is crucial. You must have tunnel vision and focus on playing one point at a time. By learning to isolate each point, you'll minimize distractions and be able to execute your strokes and strategy more effectively. It will also help to calm your nerves.

The Psychological Traps of a Tiebreaker

Many players view a tiebreaker as simply another game. In fact, that's the way it's recorded, 7-6. The truth is from a psychological standpoint, there's a huge difference.

To win a tiebreaker, you have to win at least seven points. In a super-breaker, you have to win at least 10. That's much different from the four points needed to win a game, although some games can take five or more points to win. Therefore, a tiebreaker is a longer battle tactically, mentally, and physically. Understanding this important difference will help you avoid two of the most common tiebreaker traps: relaxing when you get ahead and panicking when you fall behind.

If you win the first three points in a game, you're up 40-0 and likely to win the game. Winning the first three points in a tiebreaker doesn't have the same significance. It may feel like a big lead, but you still have a long way to go to get to seven. With that in mind, when you have the lead in a tiebreaker, do not let up.

Maintain or, if possible, increase your focus. The fact that you're a few points ahead puts extra pressure on your opponent. Take advantage of that by continuing to play high-percentage tennis. Don't give him any free points that may let him think he can come back.

On the other hand, if your opponent jumps out to an early lead, don't panic. He still has a long way to go to close out the set. Your goal: Put together three or four points in a row of your own to reverse the momentum. If you can do that, then your opponent may start to question himself, play more tentatively, and open the door for your comeback.

Tiebreaker Strategy

If you're playing at the 3.5 level or below, virtually all tiebreakers will be decided by unforced errors. That being the case, your primary strategy is to put a lot of balls back in play and see if your opponent will self-destruct.

When you're serving, get your first serve in—particularly if you're serving the first point of the tiebreaker. At the start, everyone's nervous. By getting your first serve in, you've immediately increased the pressure on your opponent. Now, he has to hit the ball in the court or lose the point.

If you miss the first serve of the tiebreaker, your opponent will get an immediate psychological lift knowing that he'll be returning your second serve. Your goal, in the tiebreaker, should be to get your first serve in play ninety percent of the time.

If you've developed your serve to the point where you can consistently hit different areas of the service box, serve to the receiver's weaker side. If you're not confident in your ability to hit different spots, aim for the center of the service box and try to serve deep in the box.

When you're receiving, try to get every serve back. It doesn't matter how weak or ugly your return may be. Put the ball back in play and make your opponent hit another shot. The highest-percentage returns, in both singles and doubles, are crosscourt. The tiebreaker is not the time to get creative and try low-percentage shots.

If your opponent misses his first serve, move forward a few inches and take a step to the side favoring your stronger stroke. Make the server think. When the weaker second serve comes, step forward, hit an aggressive (but not reckless) return and move to the net.

When the ball is in play, commit to using the high-percentage tennis strategies we've outlined earlier in this book.

> *The tiebreaker is not the place to find a new stroke or strategy. Go with the shots that brought you to the tiebreaker. If you don't own it, you can't rent it, so stay away from it.*
>
> **– Geoff Norton**
> **USTA Teaching Professional**

If you play at the 4.0 level or above, errors will still decide most points, but you'll need to take the initiative, dictate play, and force your opponent into missing.

By the time you've reached a tiebreaker, you should have figured out your opponent's strengths, weaknesses, and equally important, their tendencies. Now is the time to take advantage of all you've learned. If his backhand return of serve is weaker, repeatedly serve to his backhand. If his forehand volley is shaky, when he attacks the net, direct shots to his forehand side.

Again, remember that most players will hit the same shot, in a given situation, almost every time—it's the shot they're most confident in. When the tiebreaker comes, remind yourself of your opponent's tendencies. Where does he serve on big points? When you attack the net on his forehand side, does he try to pass you crosscourt or down the line? Recognizing and exploiting these tendencies can often help you win the tiebreaker.

I saw a great example of this recently when two players, Lance and Steve, faced each other in a USTA singles match. Throughout the match, Lance had paid strict attention to Steve's patterns and noticed that on big points Steve hit his backhand passing shots crosscourt.

When the third-set tiebreaker reached 7-6 in Steve's favor, Lance attacked the net. He hit a poor approach shot that landed short to Steve's backhand. Steve moved forward to hit the easy backhand passing shot to win the match. Just before he struck the ball, Lance, remembering Steve's tendency, quickly moved to cover the crosscourt shot. Staying true to form, Steve drove his topspin passing shot crosscourt, giving Lance an easy volley to end the point.

A few weeks later, Steve and Lance faced each other again but this time Lance held the match point. Again, Steve drove his passing shot crosscourt, and again, Lance, anticipated correctly, won the point—and the match. That little piece of information that Lance had picked up, and actually written down during a changeover, paid off in a big way.

Practice Playing Tiebreakers

Just as you develop confidence in your strokes and ability to execute certain strategies through repetition, you should include playing tiebreakers in every practice session.

Be sure to play both the seven-point and ten-point super tiebreakers. Play tiebreaker matches: two out of three or three out of five. Play them from different stages. For example, start with the tiebreaker score at 3-all or 4-all. Start up 3-0 and then down 0-3. Play tiebreakers leading 6-4 or trailing 4-6 and every score in between. To add a bit more pressure, play with each player only getting one serve.

These different starting points will help give you a sense of how each situation feels as well as force you to figure out what you need to do to close out tiebreakers or come from behind to win them. Your goal is to become comfortable with any situation that might arise. Doing so will give you tremendous confidence when tiebreaker time arrives.

Chapter 27
Adjust Your Game to the Elements

Tennis is a game of perpetual adjustment. During every match, you'll make thousands of small adjustments to strike the ball. You'll also adjust your strategy according to your opponent's style of play, the court surface, and the score. These adjustments can easily be practiced.

One of the biggest challenges, however, occurs when you face two opponents—the player on the other side of the net and Mother Nature. Whether it's wind, sun, heat, or cold, the elements can wreak havoc on your game. Yet, with the right approach, they can all be used to your advantage.

On days when Mother Nature takes the court, mental strength is a must. Players who are mentally fragile, especially those who love to make excuses, have a built-in reason for their poor play. Rather than accepting the conditions and adjusting, they fall apart. Mentally tough players accept the conditions and make the necessary psychological, technical, and tactical adjustments.

The next time you find yourself facing challenging conditions, immediately commit to the following:

- **Accept** that you won't be able to play your best tennis. You're going to make more errors. When they occur, let them go, and move on to the next point.
- **Simplify** your strategy. Aim for bigger targets to give you more margin for error.
- **Realize** that your opponent is in the same situation as you and vow to be the tougher player, both mentally and physically.

Here are a few tips to help you deal with Mother Nature's greatest weapons.

Wind

Playing tennis in a strong wind means one thing: unpredictability. You can be fully prepared to swing your racket only to have a strong gust of wind abruptly blow the ball to a completely different spot. On windy days, keep the following technical tips in mind:

- Pay extra attention to your footwork. Remind yourself to take more small adjusting steps so that you can deal with any last-second surprises.
- Shorten all of your strokes. On a windy day, long strokes can lead to more mishits and errors. With shorter strokes, last-second adjustments are easier to make.
- Overheads can be particularly challenging on a windy day. If your opponent hits a very high lob, let it bounce. This will give you more time to adjust. The ball will also bounce lower and there'll be less interference from the wind.
- When serving, slightly lower your toss. If the wind blows your toss off course, catch the ball and start over. You can do this as many times as you like.

Strategically, your first task is to identify which direction the wind is blowing:

- Is it blowing in your face?
- Is the wind at your back?
- Is it moving across your body? If so, is it moving from right to left or from left to right?

Each scenario affects your game in a different way and requires specific adjustments.

When the Wind Is Blowing Into Your face

This means that your opponent has the wind at his back, so his shots will be moving faster as they come toward you. Be extra quick with your preparation.

To absorb his increased power as well as avoid getting blown off the baseline (no pun intended), move forward and take more balls on the rise. This will not only help you to stay in the rally, but it will also take time away from your opponent.

Hitting into the wind will decrease your power. Many players view this as a free pass to become more aggressive and swing harder. Often, they go too far, overhit, and commit errors. Instead, when hitting from the baseline with the wind blowing in your face, use a little less topspin and increase your net clearance by two to four feet to maintain your shot's depth. Focus on lengthening your stroke and driving completely through the ball.

Finally, trying to hit big serves into the wind will largely be a waste of time. The wind will dramatically slow down your big serve. Forget about going for aces and service winners. Focus on spin and placement.

When the Wind Is at Your Back

With the wind at your back, your shots will automatically gain power. It's easy to be seduced into thinking you can hit even harder, a recipe for over-hitting. In this scenario, slice and topspin are your best friends. Hitting with slice will keep your balls low and make them skid quickly through the court. Topspin will help the ball drop into the court and bounce up high. Both spins are great for moving your opponent around the court as well as keeping the ball in play. Here are a few more tips for playing with the wind.

- When hitting groundstrokes. Aim two to four feet shorter than your usual targets. Let the wind provide additional depth.
- When serving. The wind will make your flat serve more powerful so you can swing a little easier to help raise your first-serve percentage. Slice serves will also be extremely effective.
- When receiving serve. Resist the urge to go for the big return. Instead, aim two to four feet shorter than your usual targets to ensure that you keep the ball in the court.

When the Wind Is Blowing Laterally

First, you need to determine which way the wind is blowing. Is it blowing from left to right or right to left? Once you've figured that out, hit your shots against the direction the wind is blowing. This means that:

- If the wind is blowing from your right to your left, hit your forehands toward the center of the court or down the line and your backhands toward the center of the court or crosscourt.
- If the wind is blowing from your left to your right, do the opposite: Hit backhands down the line and to the center and forehands to the center and cross-court.

On a windy day, attack the net. Volleys are easier to hit than groundstrokes. Plus, it will be extremely difficult for your opponent to hit accurate passing shots and lobs.

Finally, as your match moves along, be sure to constantly reassess the wind's direction and intensity (it will likely change) so that you can make the necessary adjustments.

Heat and Sun

Playing in extreme heat has caused many a player to fall apart. Here are a few strategies to help you battle each of these elements.

1. Stay Hydrated

The general rule is to take in as much liquid as you lose through sweat—approximately 32-85 ounces per hour on the court. Drink cold liquids as they're absorbed by the body faster and are more refreshing. Before your match, fill a small cooler with ice and the drink of your choice.

Remember to drink before you become thirsty. By the time your body tells you it needs a drink, it's too late. Your performance likely will have begun to decline before you feel thirsty at all. Drink at regular intervals whether you feel like it or not. Stay away from alcohol the night before a match and skip your morning caffeine. Both dehydrate your body.

2. Dress Appropriately

Stay away from dark colors. White and light-colored clothing absorbs less heat which will help you stay cool. Clothing that is light and has mesh panels will let air flow through them, lessening the chance that you'll overheat. Also, be sure to wear a hat (or visor) and wristbands. The hat will help to block the sun and you can use wristbands to wipe sweat from your face.

3. Shorten the Points—or Lengthen Them

Long baseline rallies will tire you out—quickly. Look for opportunities to move to the net so that you can end points sooner. Or, if you feel you're fitter than your opponent, do the opposite—extend the points. Keep the ball in play, move your opponent around the court, and hit drop shots and moonballs. Win the battle of attrition.

4. Stay in the Shade as Much as Possible

Some facilities have small gazebos adjacent to courts, while others have tables with umbrellas. During changeovers, you can also drape a towel over your head. For a great cooling effect, place a plastic bag filled with ice cubes on your head. Some players even pour cold water over their head and on the back of their wrists to refresh themselves. If you split sets and have a ten-minute break, rest in shade to re-energize yourself.

Sun

Your first priority when playing in the sun is to apply sunscreen. Use a water-resistant or sport-designed brand. The USTA recommends applying sunscreen thirty minutes prior to going out in the sun and suggests using a minimum of 30 SPF.

During your time on the court, your sunscreen will be washed off by sweat. Be sure to re-apply it every two to three hours. Don't forget those hard-to-reach spots like your ears, neck, shoulders, and the back of your legs.

Some players are reluctant to use sunscreen because it's a hassle to put on and they feel it affects their play. Short-term comfort isn't worth the risk of long-term skin damage. Put the sunscreen on!

Without question, the most frequent complaint I hear from players in regard to playing in the sun is how it hampers their serve and overhead. Here are two strategies to try when serving into the sun:

1. Adjust your position at the baseline. Many players get into the habit of serving from only one spot. Moving a few steps to the left or right might allow you to use your same grooved toss. If this doesn't help, try slightly changing your stance. Turning your body more toward the court, or more toward the sideline, might allow you to comfortably toss and see the ball.
2. Adjust your toss. When all else fails, try moving your toss to the right, left, over your head, more in front or lower. Keep in mind that you'll need to adjust your swing. If none of this helps, surprise your opponent with an underhand serve.

When hitting overheads into a blinding sun, try the following:

1. If possible, let the ball bounce. The ball won't rise as high after bouncing which means that you likely won't be looking directly into the sun.
2. As you prepare your racket, block as much of the sun as you can with your non-dominant hand to hit a more comfortable overhead.

By the way, don't view the sun as only a problem. Learn to use it as a weapon against your opponents. If the sun is at your back, throw up a few moonballs in the middle of a groundstroke rally. When your opponent charges the net, instead of hitting a passing shot, throw up a lob and then another and another. Forcing your opponent to continually look into the sun will break him down both physically and mentally!

Cold

Many avid tennis players, who live in cold climates and don't have access to indoor courts continue to play outdoors during the winter. Some even shovel snow off the court so they can get their practice in. Here are a few tips to keep in mind if you're one of those winter warriors.

1. Wear the Proper Clothing

Start your play with several thin, long-sleeved layers of clothing, preferably thermal underwear. As your body begins to warm, you can gradually strip away the layers. Stay away from heavy, bulky tops and bottoms. Both can hinder your movement.

Don't forget your hands. The colder your hands are, the more difficult it will be to hold your racket and make grip changes. Some players like to wear gloves to keep their hands warm. An online search will help you find products designed to do the same.

Finally, be sure to wear a hat—you lose approximately fifty percent of your body heat from your head. I've even seen some players wear earmuffs. They say that, though they can't hear the ball being struck as well, the added warmth is well worth it.

2. Lower Your String Tension

Extremely cold weather will impact the way the ball bounces. The rubber of the ball will harden, the air pressure inside the ball drops, and the ball won't bounce as high.

With a harder ball and lower bounce, generating pace will be a challenge. To combat that, try stringing your racket two pounds lower during the cold winter months.

3. Warm Up Properly

On cold days, it takes your body longer to get warm and loose. Before you take the court, do some aerobic warm-up exercises such as skipping rope or jumping jacks. Also, some dynamic stretching. Once you step onto the court, start slowly. Swing very methodically and extend your arms out on all of your strokes. This will help continue to stretch your body. Whether it's a practice session or fun match, take an additional five to ten minutes to warm up.

4. Stay Hydrated

Yes, even on a cold day you need to pay attention to your hydration. Your body uses water to maintain its core temperature in both summer and winter. You won't feel as thirsty playing in the cold, but your body still needs to be hydrated to perform at its best.

Drink at least one ounce of fluid during every changeover in cold weather, about a third of what you'd drink in warm weather.

5. Adjust Your Strategy

With the ball bouncing lower due to the cold, these three strategies will be very effective.

1. **Slice.** Adding slice to your groundstrokes and approach shots will keep the ball even lower and force your opponent to bend to get their racket beneath the ball which is easier said than done—particularly on a cold day.
2. **Drop shots.** With the harder ball bouncing lower, a well-hit drop shot will be brutal for your opponents to run down. Drop shot often.
3. **Flat and slice serves.** Both will force your opponent to bend. Topspin serves won't be as effective due to the heavier ball taking away much of the kick.

One final tip: Many public courts, particularly in the Northeast, take their nets down during the winter. Keep some caution tape in your tennis bag. On a warm winter day, tie the tape from net post to net post and you'll be good to go.

A Final Thought About
High-Percentage Tennis

When you make a true commitment to play high-percentage tennis, you'll cut down dramatically on your unforced errors. Your points will become longer and more fun. You'll get a better workout, and yes, you will win more matches.

That said, I'm frequently asked if there's a time *not* to play high-percentage tennis? It's an interesting question to which I always reply, "What do you think?" Frequently, the response is, "Yes, when I'm way ahead in a match. I'll play more aggressively, go for bigger shots and finish them off quickly." To which I vehemently respond: **absolutely not!**

If you're dominating a match never, ever, ever, change what you're doing. Clearly, it's working. Keep it up and win the match.

Does that mean there's *never* a time to move to a low-percentage approach? Not necessarily. Let's say you're way behind and the momentum is all with your opponent. You're likely to lose the match, so you might as well take a few chances.

That's exactly what happened in the 2011 US Open semifinals. Novak Djokovic faced two match points against Roger Federer. Federer had all of the momentum as well as the crowd behind him. Djokovic was visibly annoyed, and he later confided, "I would lie if I said I didn't think I'm going to lose."

Angry and frustrated, Novak figured he might as well go down swinging. He took an angry, low-percentage swing at his next return of serve. The ball flew across the court and barely nicked the line for a winner.

The shot pumped up Djokovic, who then raised his hands, urging the crowd to pump up the volume and give him a little love. The Serbian's winner also seemed to upset the usually unflappable Federer. Soon after, Djokovic was dancing at center court to celebrate his amazing, come-from-behind victory.

So, yes, when you're far behind and the momentum is against you, there's nothing wrong with shifting to a low-percentage approach to strategy. You've got nothing to lose, and who knows, maybe you'll come up with a few high-risk shots, get inside your opponent's head, and climb back into the match.

Part 4
The Truth About the Mental Game

For many players, their toughest opponent isn't the person standing on the other side of the net, it's the one residing between their ears. These players are their own worst enemies. They struggle with concentration and constantly beat themselves up with their internal and/or external dialogue. They criticize themselves for making too many errors and even their good shots aren't good enough. They're a nervous wreck before their matches, choke on the big points, and constantly make excuses for their poor performances.

Have you ever:

- Felt your heart beating out of your chest as you walked onto the court for a match?
- Committed a horrendous error when all you needed to do was get the ball back in the court?
- On a big point, hit your second serve into the bottom of the net?
- Blamed the sun, wind, heat, your racket, your mother, father, spouse, or even your horoscope for your latest loss?

Of course, you have—we all have. We commit those horrendous errors because we lose our concentration. Our heart pounds because we're nervous, we double fault on big points because we choke, and we make excuses because we don't want to admit that we choked. In this section of the book, we'll take a look at the battles we fight from within.

Chapter 28
Keys to Better Concentration

While most of us start our matches with a high level of concentration, something inevitably comes along to distract us. It could be a missed shot, something our partner did (or didn't do), a bad line call from our opponents, or something that happened at home earlier in the day.

Our minds are wired to be active, so to completely prevent a lapse in concentration is impossible. The key is to recognize when it's happening and then have a plan in place to bring it back to the present moment. Here are a few strategies to help you push aside the distracting thoughts and regain your concentration.

> *I believe the brain is like a muscle—like any other, it can be improved.*
>
> **– Ivan Lendl**
> **Tennis Legend**

1. Set a Goal

We lose our concentration when our mind becomes distracted by something else. To help prevent distractions, set a goal such as:

- **Your primary strategy**—playing to your opponent's backhand, attacking the net, lobbing, etc.
- **Tracking the ball**—I like to say "tracking" as opposed to "watching." Watching the ball can be done casually. Tracking the ball from your opponent's racket to yours requires sustained concentration.
- **Preparing your racket quickly**—This will both elevate your concentration and dramatically improve your shot-making.

- **Moving your feet**—A wandering mind results in lazy footwork. A focused mind produces intense feet which, in turn, means you recover quicker, get to the next ball faster, and ultimately win more matches.

2. Take Concentration Breaks

By taking brief, scheduled breaks, you'll give your mind a rest and then be able to return to a deeply focused state. These breaks can be:

- **Between points.** As soon as the point ends, take a deep breath, quickly review the point, and then let go of all thought. Walk to the back fence, focus on your breath, fix your strings, try to empty your mind. Then, to prepare for the next point, remind yourself of your primary strategy or pick a new one.
- **Between games and during changeovers.** Do the same things, except now you have more time. Review what happened during the last two games, then take a break from thinking.

If your mind simply won't calm down, keep yourself busy doing little things like breathing deeply, fixing your strings, taking small sips of your drink, drying yourself with a towel, etc.

When you learn to empty your mind and give yourself a concentration break, you'll be able to mentally reset and return to a deep state of focus when the next point begins.

3. Monitor Your Concentration

Become aware of the ebbs and flows of your concentration. Every few games, ask yourself, "On a scale of 1 (low) to 3 (high), how well am I concentrating?" If your concentration is low, raise it by reminding yourself of your goals. Eventually, you'll become more attuned to your level of concentration and know how to sharpen it when needed.

> *Competitive toughness is an acquired skill and not an inherited gift.*
>
> **– Chris Evert**
> **Tennis Legend**

The distracting thoughts will never go away, but your relationship with them can change. You'll learn to become aware of them and elect not to engage. Instead, you'll be able to refocus your mind on something that will help you win the match.

One final tip for improving your concentration: take off your electronic watch at the start of the match. I've seen players receive texts in the middle of a point and glance at their watch.

Not only is this a bad idea from a tennis perspective, you also might get hurt! Put your watch in your bag; if you must check it, do so between games.

Chapter 29
Choking (Everyone Does It)

We choke because we're afraid. Afraid to lose. Afraid of looking bad in front of our friends. Afraid of letting our team down. Some players are even afraid to win because they'll be expected to win again. Who needs that pressure?

Choking is the end result of being nervous. Pounding heart, dry mouth, tightness in the belly. These are just a few of the symptoms of nerves on the tennis court. Everyone feels them—even the pros.

Nervousness is an emotion that can't be eliminated any more than happiness or sadness. While a certain amount of nervousness is a good thing (it means you care) being overly nervous can cause you to shift into panic mode. You play too fast, become tense, try low-percentage shots to end points quickly, and yes, you choke!

> *To avoid moments of panic or deal with them when they arise, first take a deep breath as you prepare to serve or receive serve.*
>
> *– Ken Dehart*

We've all choked and anyone who tells you they haven't is lying. However, winning players have developed techniques to minimize choking. The next time you feel the pressure building, here are a few ideas to help keep your heart from exploding and your grip dry:

- **Breathe.** Become aware of your breath as it goes in and out. A common response to nerves is to hold our breath. That only makes our muscles tighten up even more. Make sure to breathe in as you prepare your racket and, as you make contact, breathe out. Grunting is also a great way to release tension.

- **Keep your feet moving.** Footwork is one of the first things to go when we get nervous. When you begin to feel tight, bounce up and down and side to side. The constant movement will help you stay loose as well as maintain your concentration.

- **Relax your hand.** When we get nervous, we tend to hold our racket in a death grip. Keep your fingers loose until just before you strike the ball. In between points, hold your racket in your non-dominant hand to relax your hitting arm.

> *Pressure is a privilege, it's what you do with it that matters.*
>
> **– Billie Jean King**
> **Tennis Legend**

- **Say "bounce, hit."** Tim Gallwey, in his groundbreaking book, *The Inner Game of Tennis*, suggests that players say *"bounce"* to themselves when the ball touches the court, and *"hit"* when the ball makes contact with their racket. This mantra will automatically quiet your mind as well as take your focus off how nervous you are. It will also improve your timing.

- **Visualize the next point.** Visualization is a mental rehearsal that produces both positive images and emotions. The next time you step to the line to serve at six-all in the third set tiebreaker and feel your legs beginning to shake, step away from the line, take a deep breath, and internally go through the point:

> *"I'm going to serve out wide, follow it to the net,*
> *and hit my first volley to the open court."*

When you visualize a positive outcome, you increase the likelihood of that outcome occurring.

- **Forget the future.** Choking occurs because of ifs. We think, "If I lose this next point, I'm in trouble," or "If I lose this match, what will my friends say?" Instead of worrying about what may happen in the future, put your attention on the present moment. During the point, focus on the ball. Once the point ends, concentrate on your breathing and your strategy for the next point. If you feel an "if" creeping into your mind, push it aside with a deep breath.

And perhaps the best advice to conquer your nerves is to **play more matches**. The more matches you play, the more familiar you'll become with the experience and less nervous you'll be.

Chapter 30
Negativity and Excuses

"My serve is horrible."
"I move like an elephant."
"I can't believe I'm losing to him. I stink!"

Many players have become experts at putting themselves down. They're uncomfortable with praise and particularly adept at accentuating the negative.

Negative self-talk affects your level of effort and can often become a self-fulfilling prophecy. When you say to yourself, "I stink," you'll go after balls half-heartedly, your strokes will deteriorate, and before you know it, you *do* stink!

Here are a few strategies to help you silence your inner critic and use self-talk to your advantage.

- **Become aware of your thoughts.** Pay attention to the messages you're sending yourself. Some players journal, writing down negative thoughts. They're then able to see how many times they put themselves down. Sadly, some players fill up several notebooks.

- **Break the pattern.** When you feel a negative thought creeping in, take a deep breath and immediately say, "No! I am not going to do this." It sounds simplistic, but it works.

- **Be positive.** Stop the flow of negativity with a few positive, constructive statements. Instead of telling yourself how slow or lazy you are, try saying something like

> *So many adults I see are serious about improving but are so self-critical and negative that they get in their own way. If they could only learn to have fun and enjoy the process, it would go a long way toward helping them achieve their goals.*
>
> **– Rick Macci**

"Come on, you can get to those. Get up on your toes, split step, and run for every ball until it bounces twice." Or, after an unforced error, remind yourself to "keep your eyes on the point of contact." Positive thoughts are vital because if you say it enough, you will believe it.

- **Observe without judging.** This means being aware of what's happening on the court without criticizing yourself. For example, if you've hit your last three serves into the net, rather than getting upset, remind yourself that you have a tendency to drop your head as you serve. Make the correction, tell yourself that you've "got it now," and eagerly move on to the next point.

Dr. John F. Murray, the author of *Smart Tennis*, has devised a great experiment to help monitor self-talk. The next time you walk onto the court, place forty paper clips in your right pocket. Each time you catch yourself making a negative comment, reach into your pocket and transfer one paperclip to the left pocket. At the end of the match, see how many clips have gone to the left side. You might be shocked and motivated to change.

> *While adversity is inevitable, negative thinking is optional.*
>
> *– Tom Veneziano*
> *Tennis Teaching Professional*

Work at it and gradually you'll see a change in the way you speak to, and feel about, yourself. After a month or two, try the paper clip experiment again and see how much you've improved.

By learning to think positively, you can regain the momentum and control of your mental game.

Excuses

At one time or another, we've all fallen into the trap of making excuses. After a tough loss, we blame the wind, our partner, bad calls, or even our spouse who upset us off before we left the house.

If we're taking a lesson and not getting what our pro is teaching us, it's because our elbow hurts, the teaching balls are dead, or the pro just stinks. It certainly can't be our fault.

Excuses are a transparent attempt to make others think we're better than our current performance indicates, or at the very least, to evoke some sympathy. In reality, no one buys it, and we only come across as weak and insecure.

Even worse, making excuses a habit hurts our long-term development. The more we allow ourselves to give in to the (brief) psychological comfort of making excuses, the more it allows us to rationalize our poor performance. As a result, we don't acknowledge the weaknesses in our game and don't work to improve them.

Why We Make Excuses

Whether it's playing a long, hard match or trying to learn a new technique, tennis can be stressful. The more emotionally invested we become in the result, the more stress we feel. Making excuses is a way to escape that stress.

When things go wrong on the court, you have a choice to make. You can either make excuses, or you can take responsibility for your performance and learn from it.

Those who choose to make excuses are basically saying that they have no control over their play. In doing so, they ignore valuable feedback that will ultimately make them a better player.

The next time you feel the urge to rationalize your poor performance with an excuse, bite your lip, stop feeling sorry for yourself, and keep the following in mind:

- **It's on you**. If, in your last match, you missed easy overheads or consistently double faulted, own it. If you're playing doubles, say to your partner, "My fault." When you own your performance, you're acknowledging that you're in control and have the power to improve it.
- **Learn from your mistakes.** Why did you miss those overheads and double fault so often? Sloppy preparation for the overheads? An erratic toss on the serves? Analyze what went wrong and figure out how you can do better in the future. Remember, every mistake you make is an opportunity to learn.
- **Become aware of, and then adjust, your attitude.** As with the tendency to be negative, you can change the habit of making excuses. You just have to be motivated and strong enough to do it.

Become aware of the thoughts in your mind and the words that come out of your mouth. When you feel an excuse bubbling up, take a deep breath and immediately say, "No! I am not going to do this."

"The quickest way to increase results is to decrease excuses."

These words were spoken by Roger Crawford whom _Sports Illustrated_ called "one of the most accomplished, physically challenged athletes in the history of sport."

Crawford was born with a rare genetic condition that left him with one finger on his right hand and two on his left. He had three toes on his right foot and a withered left leg, which would later have to be amputated. Doctors told Roger's parents that he would never be able to walk and would likely have to be taken care of for the rest of his life.

Rogers's parents told him that he was only as handicapped as he chose to be. They never let him feel sorry for himself and encouraged him to always do what he wanted to do, even if it might be a little more challenging.

Roger loved sports and one day picked up a Wilson T2000 tennis racket and accidentally wedged his finger between the racket's double-barreled throat. The racket fit his hand snugly and he found that he could swing the racket like an able-bodied player.

With perseverance, dedication, and countless hours on a backboard, Roger became a tennis player. He went on to play college tennis at Loyola Marymount University where he was the first Division I college athlete to compete with a disability affecting all four limbs. He finished his career with 22 wins and 11 losses.

Roger became the first physically disabled tennis player to be certified as a teaching professional by the United States Professional Tennis Association. Today, Roger tours the world as a motivational speaker and has a series of videos on the Tennis Channel called Motivational Mondays. He's also written the best-selling books: _Playing From The Heart, Think Again,_ and _How High Can You Bounce?_

You can learn more about this amazing man by going to his website: rogercrawford.com.

Chapter 31
Rituals Work

One of the best ways to combat, and even conquer, your inner opponents is through the use of rituals. Rituals help you calm your mind, manage your emotions, and navigate the ups and downs of your matches. They also provide you with a feeling of control in situations where it may seem you have none.

Many players think of rituals only when they're serving or receiving serve. The truth is rituals can help you long before you take the court and even after your matches have finished.

Pre-Match Ritual

We've all seen players who sprint onto the court five minutes after the scheduled start of the match. They apologize to their partner and opponents, complaining about whatever it was that made them late. They mindlessly hit a few balls and then become annoyed when the allotted warm-up time ends. They haven't warmed up their body, calmed their mind or sized up their opponent. Clearly, they're not ready to play.

Certainly, life can get in the way of your tennis. However, if you want to play your best, remember that your matches begin before you walk onto the court. If you design and stick to a pre-match ritual, you'll not only start your matches in a better frame of mind, you'll also be more physically prepared in case your opponents don't give you a good warmup.

> *Knowing you have done all the right things before you go to compete gives you a sense of confidence and improves your chances of playing well.*
>
> *– Ken Dehart*

Here's an example of an ideal pre-match ritual.

- Arrive at the courts 30 minutes before your scheduled match.
- Break a light sweat by hitting some tennis balls on court or even in the parking lot with a friend. Do some dynamic stretching.
- Spend a few quiet minutes alone or, if playing doubles, with your partner.
- Head to the court.

Your Rituals During the Match

Serve, return of serve, in-between points and changeover rituals help you forget about the past, bring you into the present, and reset for what's next. Here are mine:

Serving Ritual

- Bounce the ball three times.
- Take a deep breath.
- Look at my hand and racket as they come together to start my serve.
- Pause.
- Begin my service motion.

Return of Serve Ritual

- Walk back, with my eyes focused on my strings, and touch the back fence with my racket.
- Walk back toward the court, eyes still focused on my strings.
- Step into position, left foot first, then right. Head looking down at the court.
- Shift weight from my left foot to my right three times, head still down.
- Look up, signaling to my opponent that I'm ready.

Between Points

The point has ended. You now have twenty five seconds to get ready for the next. Catch your breath and let go of the stress. Turn away from your opponent and walk to the back fence.

Your mind will move to where your eyes focus, so keep your vision within the confines of the court. Place your racket in your non-dominant hand and look at your strings. Take four or five deep, controlled breaths, and as you push the air out, relax your neck and shoulders. Give yourself five to ten seconds to recover.

Take the next five to ten seconds to quickly review the previous point. Without emotion, observe why you won or lost the point. Give yourself two quick tips and then move on. For example, if your opponent beat you to the net and hit a winning volley, remind yourself to "aim higher over the net to keep the ball deeper in the court."

If he made an error on his backhand, tell yourself to "keep pounding his backhand." Keep it short and simple; you don't have time for in-depth strategizing.

With the remaining few seconds, gear up for the next point. Bounce up and down on your toes. Take a long look at your opponent and give yourself a quick tip for your next shot. If you're serving, visualize where you'll place your serve. Say to yourself, "out wide" or "into the body." If you're receiving serve, tell yourself to "focus on the ball and block it back."

Jorge Capestany has a great four-part ritual for doubles players when they're between points.

- Find your partner on the court and make eye contact.
- Come together for some type of physical touch. Tap the shoulder, bump fists, etc.
- Verbally strategize the next point.
- Reset. Come apart, sprint into position, and get ready.
- Repeat after every point.

Jorge says that "Every team that's playing well and having fun is doing this. The exact opposite is those two ships in the night. The net player walks to the other side, the server does the same. They never come together, and the fun factor is way down." I'll add that they also win very few matches.

The Changeover

During the changeover, you have ninety seconds before the next game begins. Andre Agassi used to sprint to his chair as soon as the changeover began. You should as well. Towel off your arms, legs, and neck.

Sip your water, close your eyes, and take five deep breaths. Use the first twenty seconds to recover from the previous two games physically and emotionally.

Over the next forty-five seconds, examine what's happening at this point in the match. Understand how and why you're winning and losing points. If you notice your opponent's backhand is landing short in the court, commit to hitting to his backhand.

If you're struggling with your forehand, design patterns that will bring more balls to your backhand. If your first-serve percentage is low, remind yourself to take some pace off and add more spin. If you're tiring, plan to shorten the points by coming to the net.

Many times, you'll be able to protect/hide your weaknesses during the match. However, take note of these weaknesses so that you can work on them in practice.

During changeovers, pay attention to your opponent's body language. Does he appear angry, frustrated, or tired? If the answer is yes, you're obviously getting to him, so stick with the strategies you've been using.

Most players will hit the same shot every time in a given situation so remind yourself of their tendencies. Where does he serve on big points? When you attack the net on his forehand side, does he try to pass crosscourt or down the line? Or does he always lob? Identifying these tendencies can help you win matches.

Finally, plan your strategy for the next two games. If you're comfortably ahead or the match is close, stick with your game plan. If you find yourself slightly behind, don't panic. Close matches are usually decided by a few points so stay the course. If you can win a few of those big points, you can easily turn the match in your favor.

If you're getting blown off the court, slow the tempo of the match. Use every one of your ninety seconds. Let your opponent walk back onto the court first and make him wait for you. Once play resumes, use the full twenty five seconds between points.

Just because your opponent may be on a hot streak, it doesn't mean he can keep it up for the full match. By making him play at your pace, you can often take him out of his rhythm and turn the match around.

Post-Match Ritual

Your attention should immediately turn to recovery—physically, mentally, and emotionally. The following tips will help your body begin to recover and get you ready for your next match.

- Take a light jog or hop on a stationary bike.
- Do some static stretching.
- Have a massage.
- Take an ice bath or cold shower.
- Refuel your body.

The National Academy of Sports Medicine says that your post-match goal is to eat foods and drink fluids that replenish muscle glycogen, fluids, and electrolytes lost during the match. They suggest the following:

- As you walk off the court, drink a sports drink. This will help you to replenish the body fluids lost during the match.
- Eat complex carbohydrates as soon as possible, preferably within 30 minutes of a match.
- Consume a high-carbohydrate meal that also contains a lean protein source (e.g., yogurt and fruit, peanut butter and apple) within two hours after play to maximize muscle glycogen replenishment and muscle protein synthesis.

You can also use this time to reflect on the match. What did you do well? What did you do poorly? What do you need to work on in your next lesson?

If you've just finished a doubles match and you both agree, sit down with your partner and discuss the match. Do this while things are still fresh in your mind. If you've lost a tough match and emotions are running high, go your separate ways for a while. When enough time has passed, come back together and talk about the match.

Many players (and teams) keep notes on their various opponents. They record the score, the opponent's strengths, weaknesses, and tendencies as well as what strategies worked and what didn't. When they face that opponent in the future, they have a nice head start on their preparation.

Design your own before, during, and after match rituals. Use them when you practice so that they become second nature when you play matches. Rituals work.

Part 5
The Truth About Improvement

Another USTA season had ended for John, exactly the same way as the previous three—a losing record and a drop in his rating.

In John's last match, he faced Bobby, a soft-hitting, lower-rated player that he knew he could beat easily. John walked onto the court, popped the top off the can of balls, confident that he would end an otherwise lousy season with a win.

Sixty minutes later, John left the court a straight-sets loser. All he had to show for his efforts was a can of used balls, a sore arm, and a perfunctory "good match" comment from Bobby. To make matters worse, John knew that what Bobby really meant to say was "Ha! I've been playing tennis three years less than you, and I won."

John's fuming. He goes through the usual list of excuses that creep into everyone's mind immediately after a bad loss: "The sun was in my eyes, my racket was strung too loose, he cheated, my pro stinks..." These rationalizations temporarily eased John's pain.

By the time he'd showered, reclaimed his rackets from the trash can, and settled into his car for the long ride home, John forced himself to face a disturbing reality. In the past three years, his game has not improved one bit. In fact, he might actually have gotten worse.

He has little consistency from the baseline and at net, and God forbid he misses his first serve because his second is a disaster. To make matters worse, John's arm aches all the time, his back is stiff, and he can no longer ignore the fact that his shorts are much tighter around his waist than they used to be. John had officially hit tennis' version of rock bottom and decided that he would either get serious about improving his game or quit. That's when he came to me.

There are millions of recreational players around the world who share some version of John's story. They play tennis two or three times a week. Sometimes they play well, other times they don't. Their level of play stays pretty much the same throughout their tennis lives, and there's absolutely nothing wrong with that—people enjoy the sport for different reasons.

However, if you're a player who is truly serious about improving, you need to realize that it won't happen just because you show up to the courts a few times a week. Over the next few chapters, I'm going to take you through the process of designing your personal plan for improvement.

Chapter 32
Make a Plan

If you really want to make a commitment to improving your game, you need a plan. The first step in that plan is to take a hard look at your game.

Grab a piece of paper and do a personal tennis skills inventory. Write a sentence or two about each area of your game. Be honest and focus on both your physical and mental skills. If you're working with a coach, get together with him and ask his thoughts.

When John and I sat down to do this, he told me to be "brutally honest, no matter how much it hurt." When I heard this, I was thrilled because I knew we would make progress. Unfortunately, many players come to their coaches for lessons, but they really don't want to hear the truth. If you tell them their forehand is weak, they take it as a personal affront. It isn't, it just means that their forehand is weak and needs work. As Steve Smith says, "Facts don't have feelings."

Below is the basic skills inventory that John and I put together. Yours can be as simple or as detailed as you like. We wrote this from John's perspective to make it feel more personal and put the responsibility on him.

Tennis Skills Inventory for John Watson

Forehand Groundstroke: I prepare very late and, as a result, am frequently poorly positioned. I tend to hit the ball late and far too flat. I panic under pressure and try to blast my way out of trouble.

Backhand groundstroke: My two-handed backhand is extremely erratic. My footwork is slow, and I often get too close to the ball.

Volleys: Pretty good but I tend to swing too much on both sides.

Overhead: I overhit virtually every time. I need to work on better preparation.

Serve: My toss is erratic. I always go for a big first serve, which seldom goes in. Then I can only hit a much softer version of my second serve.

Return of serve: Inconsistent. I can't handle a hard serve and frequently over-hit second serve returns.

Fitness: My agility, strength, and endurance are slightly below average for someone my age (mid-40s). Flexibility is poor. I should lose ten pounds.

Mental game: My mind wanders frequently, and I tend to get down on myself very quickly. People tell me I often appear angry on the court.

Once you've thought about and documented your strengths and weaknesses, you can come up with a plan for improvement. Vic Braden once asked Roger Federer what he did to get so good? Federer replied that he sat down and made a list of all the shots he wanted to be able to hit. You should too.

Your plan should include both short-and long-term goals. Short-term goals might be things like changing a grip, adding a new shot, or getting fitter. Your short-term goals should build to a long-term goal, such as the start of a new season or a big event.

> *You have to believe in the long-term plan you have, but you need the short-term goals to motivate and inspire you.*
>
> **– Roger Federer**

John made a very wise move when he decided to sit out his team's summer USTA season. He knew that if he played competitive matches, his focus would be more on winning than working on the skills he needed to improve. Instead, he would use the summer to rebuild his game and come back strong for the fall season. Below are the short and long-term goals that John and I came up with to get him ready for his next USTA season, three months away. Again, we wrote from John's perspective.

Goals for John Watson

Long-term goal: I want to have a winning record for the fall USTA season. To accomplish that, I'm setting the following **short-term goals**:

- I will become more consistent from all areas of the court.
- I will become fitter, faster, and more flexible.
- I will improve my mental game.

After determining John's goals, we did a few lessons so I could outline some technical changes that I felt he needed to make. We continued weekly lessons throughout the summer.

Once you've set your short and long-term goals, you need to decide what you're going to do to achieve them. This is your course of action. See John's plan below.

Course of Action

Short-term goal: To become more consistent.

Course of action: I will practice at least three times a week with another player. I'll do groundstroke consistency drills. I need to develop the ability to keep the ball in play for an extended period of time, so I'll hit at whatever pace I need to keep the ball going. I'll supplement these practice sessions by working with a ball machine and/or hitting against a backboard. I must be sure to focus on the early preparation I've worked on during my lessons.

Every time I practice, I hit at least one basket of serves to become more comfortable with the grip change I made. I'll set up targets in the service box and remind myself that consistency and control are more important than power.

Short-term goal: Become fitter, faster, and more flexible.

Course of action: I'll immediately begin both on and off-court fitness programs, including endurance and agility exercises.

Endurance: I'll run or walk for 30 minutes, three times a week, going as fast or as slow as I need to complete the time. If necessary, I'll gradually build up to 30 minutes.

> **Agility:** I'll jump rope on the days I don't do my endurance training. I'll begin by jumping with both feet, and then just the left foot, then the right, and then alternating feet. I'll build up to the following:
>
> > 25 jumps with both feet.
> > 25 jumps on the left foot.
> > 25 jumps on the right foot.
> > 25 jumps alternating feet.
>
> **Diet:** I'm going to drink more water, eat more nutritious food, stay away from junk food, and eat nothing in the three hours before I go to bed.
>
> **Flexibility:** I commit to doing tennis-specific stretches twice a day, every day.
>
> **Short-term goal:** Improve my mental game.
>
> **Course of action:** I'm going to spend ten minutes a day listening to the meditation app we found to improve my focus. Also, I'll practice deep breathing exercises for five minutes a day for use as an on-court calming technique.

Before John went to work, I gave him two final suggestions that I'll pass along to you as well.

1. Start a Tennis Journal

In it, John kept his skills inventory and goals sheets. He took notes during our lessons, planned, and recorded his practice and workout sessions, and jotted down any thoughts or questions that came to mind as he played or practiced. You can buy an actual journal or design your own. It doesn't matter, as long as you put your thoughts and goals down on paper. The more planning and thought you give to your game, the faster you'll improve.

2. Study the Game

John also began to read books and watch videos by tennis experts to deepen his understanding of the techniques and strategies that make a winning player. You should as well. You'll find anything by Vic Braden, Dennis Van der Meer, Peter Burwash, Jorge Capestany and Steve Smith both interesting and educational.

> *One of my favorite tools for players is to begin with journaling. Just start journaling. Say you pick three times in a day, and you just journal your thoughts. What are you thinking about? What are those repetitive thoughts? Journaling helps one to become more self-aware.*
>
> **– Emma Doyle**
> **High Performance Coach**

With his plan in place, John went to work. Every few weeks, we sat down and evaluated his progress. We checked off the small goals he achieved and added new ones as he moved closer to his fall season.

Along the way, John suffered the ups, downs, and frustrations that we all do on the path to improvement. To his enormous credit, he persevered, achieved his goals, and has had winning records—and improved ratings—his last two USTA seasons. Today, John is not only a much better player he's also a much happier person.

Chapter 33
There's Only One Way

How many times a week do you practice? I don't mean five minutes of casual mini tennis, a few groundstrokes, and then a "first one in" set. I'm talking about walking onto the court with a specific plan to maximize your time, hit a lot of balls, and work on various aspects of your game.

I'm sure you're busy and the time you can set aside for tennis is at a premium. Playing sets and matches is fun—and certainly one element of practice—but it's not the best use of on-court time because the ball is generally not in play for very long.

If you're serious about improving your tennis, at least once a week step onto the court with a set of drills that will allow you to hit as many balls as possible and work on your game.

Practice with the same focus and intensity that you bring to your matches. Chase down and hit every ball with energy and purpose. Tennis Hall of Famer Mats Wilander once said to me that he doesn't understand how people go to the gym or an exercise class after they've played tennis. "If you've worked as hard as you should on the tennis court, you should be tired when you're finished playing," said Mats.

> *My idea of intensive practice is to pick out one stroke and hammer away at that shot until it is completely mastered.*
>
> **– Bill Tilden**
> **Tennis Legend**

Practice What Needs Practice

Every tennis player knows that they should work on their weaknesses. However, many players spend most of their time working on their strengths, paying little (if any) attention to the weaknesses in their game. I get it: working on what you're already good at is easier and it feels great. However, as your strengths become stronger, your weaknesses will still be there and cost you matches.

They go through the session with the same sloppy footwork and poor technique that they exhibit in matches. All this accomplishes is reinforcing their bad habits. Steve Smith says that these players are "practicing getting better at getting worse." Identify your weaknesses and commit yourself to improving them.

An online search will provide you with hundreds of drills that can help you work on every aspect of your game. Below, I've put together a very basic practice program that will take you through all aspects of your game. Be sure to warm up your body before taking the court. You don't want to waste valuable court time getting loose. Bring a basket or several cans of balls to minimize pick-up time.

- **Mini tennis, inside the service lines.** Two minutes.
- **Full-court rally, lengthening your strokes.** Three minutes.
- **Crosscourt forehands.** Five minutes.
- **Crosscourt backhands.** Five minutes.
- **Down the line groundstrokes.** Standing at the baseline, on your deuce side, practice hitting down the line forehands. Your training partner, standing on his ad side, practices down the line backhands. Reverse after five minutes.
- **Reflex volleys from the service lines.** Five minutes.
- **Groundstroke/volley rally.** One player at the net, the other at the baseline. Switch after five minutes.
- **Overhead/lob rally.** The player at the baseline hits only lobs while the player at the net returns with overheads. Switch after five minutes.
- **Serve and return.** One player serves, the other returns away from the server. Switch after five minutes.
- **Play practice points.** Pick something to work on during the points, such as attacking the net or serving to different areas of the box. Don't worry about who wins the points. As Roger Federer once said, when asked about losing to players in practice:

"I didn't know you were supposed to win when practicing."

What If I Have No One to Practice With?

Find a wall or backboard. Fifteen minutes on a backboard is equivalent to one hour on the court in terms of the number of balls hit. I prefer backboards to ball machines because what you hit to the wall, will be reflected by what comes back to you. "Garbage in, garbage out" is how one of my players put it. If you can consistently control the ball hitting against a backboard, you've truly accomplished something. See below for a backboard practice program.

- Stand approximately eight feet from the backboard and gently hit forehand groundstrokes. Pick a specific spot on the wall or tape up a square to use as a target. Take short swings and hit the ball on one bounce. Try to keep it going as many times as you can. Five minutes.
- Switch to gentle backhand groundstrokes. Five minutes.
- Then, alternate between forehand and backhand groundstrokes. Five minutes.
- Take nine more steps away from the backboard. This will put you approximately 39 feet from the wall, the distance from the net to the baseline. Repeat the first exercise, increasing the size of your swing to hit a full forehand groundstroke. Five minutes.
- Backhands. Five minutes.
- Alternate between forehands and backhands. Five minutes.
- Take ten steps forward, which should place you about nine feet from the wall. Practice your forehand volleys for five minutes.
- Backhand volleys. Five minutes.
- Alternate between forehand and backhand volleys for five minutes.
- Practice overheads by hitting the ball off the ground close to the wall, so that it bounces off the backboard high in the air. Five minutes.
- For the next five minutes, move from one area to the other. Starting at the baseline distance from the wall, hit five forehand and then five backhand (full swing) groundstrokes. Then move up a few feet and hit five forehand and five backhand (smaller swing) groundstrokes. Finally, move to the net position and hit five forehand and then five backhand volleys, without letting the ball bounce. Try to complete the entire cycle without missing.
- Serve for five minutes. Aim for various spots on the wall.

If you find it difficult to keep the ball going with groundstrokes or volleys, try using the lower compression green or orange transition balls. They will slow down the pace to help you develop your rhythm.

Be patient and expect to struggle to control the ball. These drills focus on the fundamentals which is what *everyone* needs to improve. Even Roger Federer, when going through a rough patch, frequently said that he needed to "get back to the fundamentals."

What If There's No Wall Available?

Shadow swinging allows you to dramatically slow down, and deeply focus on your strokes. Golfers do it, baseball players do it, and you should too. Stand in front of a mirror and take five to ten slow, methodical shadow swings for each stroke. Do it every day. It will take you less than five minutes, yet it will strengthen the connection between your brain and body and improve your technique dramatically.

> *If you don't practice, you don't deserve to win.*
>
> **– Andre Agassi**

Chapter 34
How to Improve Your USTA Rating

The last chapter gave you some very general practice plans and drills that will help you improve all your strokes. Both are evergreen, and you should do them throughout your tennis life.

However, if you're a serious USTA player hoping to improve your rating, you need to set more specific goals and design practice plans to achieve them. The first step is to understand that the strokes and strategies that won matches for you at the 3.0 level won't get it done at the 4.0 level and above.

In this chapter, I'm going to go through the escalating USTA ratings from the perspective of the skills you'll need to develop to reach that next level. As you plan your climb up the ratings ladder, decide on an ultimate goal. Make it realistic. Consider where you are in your life and how much time you'll be able to devote to your game.

As you move along, always keep your end goal in mind. This is crucial because, as you work to develop your new skills, your frustration level will rise. Your overall level of play will drop, and you'll likely lose to players that you once beat easily.

Pete Sampras was a great example of this. When Sampras was one of the top 14-and-under players in the country, his coach, Pete Fischer, had him abandon his two-handed backhand—what Sampras called "my best shot."

> *USTA league tennis can create a lot of pressure for players with the lineups and perceived judgment related to winning and losing. It is important for players to find perspective, focus on what they can control on the court, have specific goals when they play beyond the outcome so they can feel good on the court. It is possible to enjoy the matches, be good sports and still play competitively.*
>
> **– Jeff Greenwald**

Fischer knew that as good as Pete's backhand was in the junior game, it ultimately wouldn't be strong enough for the pros.

With the end goal of pro tennis greatness in mind, Fischer had Sampras switch to a one-handed backhand. Pete soon began losing to players that, prior to the change, couldn't stay on the court with him. His new backhand was simply too erratic. However, he persevered with the one-hander and the rest is history.

Regularly remind yourself of the rating you aspire to reach and the skills you'll need to get there. In the process of developing those skills, you'll struggle and often be tempted to revert to your comfort zone. Don't! Stay the course.

Below is an overview of what I feel your primary improvement goals should be to get from one rating level to the next. I'm going to focus on the 3.0-4.5 levels because that's where most recreational players roam.

3.0–3.5: Technical

3.5–4.0: Tactical

4.0–4.5: Physical

Moving from 3.0–3.5

If you're playing at the 3.0 level, continue to develop the technical aspects of your game. Keep these primary points in mind:

- Begin in the proper ready position and return to it after each shot.
- Make the split step a habit.
- Prepare your racket as quickly as possible.
- Create the proper space between you and the ball.
- Keep your eye on the point of contact for one recovery step after all your shots.

Fact is, 3.5-level players are more consistent than 3.0s and, as a result, their points are longer. Focusing on the above technical tips will improve your consistency as will drills like those outlined in the previous chapter.

If you're able to take private lessons, spend time refining your technique, developing new shots, and improving your overall consistency.

Become comfortable using the continental grip. It will allow you to do many things with the ball that you'll need as you advance to the higher levels.

Moving from 3.5–4.0

As a 3.5, you've developed your strokes and can play with a decent level of consistency. Continue to refine the technical aspects of your game. To move to the 4.0 level, however, you need to make strategy and shot selection the primary focus.

Many 3.5 player's approach to strategy relies on the big shot. They've learned to hit the ball harder and often feel that because they can, they always should. Their 3.5-level opponents aren't yet skilled enough to handle the harder ball, so the strategy often works.

Plus, because 3.5s haven't yet ingrained the proper movement and anticipation skills, there are a lot of open areas on the court to exploit. The end result is that many points at the 3.5 level are won by hitting the ball too hard, and to the wrong place. This approach *will not work* at the next level.

Those open areas will no longer be open, and a 4.0-level player's technical skills have evolved to the point where your big shots won't phase them. To move to the 4.0 level, you'll need to learn how to actually play the game.

A 4.0 player is more patient and intelligent. He understands high-percentage shot selection, court positioning, and when to play offense or shift to defense. He's accepted that tennis is a game of errors and built his strategies around that fact.

To reach this level, focus on implementing the high-percentage strategies outlined earlier in the book in both your practice sessions and matches. If you're able to take lessons with a qualified pro, do what are called situation drills. This is where the pro will create specific situations where you can practice the proper shot selection and positioning skills. For example, the pro feeds you three balls.

First ball: A deep groundstroke. Return it crosscourt, deep.

Second ball: A short ball. Move forward and hit it straight ahead. Then move to the net, following the ball.

Third ball: A volley. Hit your volley crosscourt into the open court.

This is a basic shot combination that, if well-executed, will win you many singles points at the 4.0 level.

There are an endless number of singles and doubles situation drills your pro—or you and a practice partner—can create to help you practice the high-percentage shot patterns that win at the 4.0 level.

Again, accept that you're going to miss a lot of shots and lose many points during this process. The skills you're trying to develop aren't yet natural, so there'll always be that moment of hesitation. Remind yourself that you're practicing and always keep your end goal in mind. Practice playing the game the way it's played at the level you want to reach.

Moving from 4.0–4.5

If you've reached the 4.0 level, let me congratulate you. You are truly a better tennis player than the vast majority of those who play the game. Now, what do you need to improve to reach the 4.5 level? Pretty much everything.

You'll need to hit the ball harder, deeper, and with more spin and precision. You'll have to react sooner, move around the court more efficiently, and recover faster between shots.

Moving up in the ratings gets more difficult with each step. The move from 3.5–4.0 is twice as hard as going from 3.0 to 3.5. Moving from 4.0–4.5 will be even more challenging.

There is where you need to pause and give yourself a reality check. As I said in Truth #1: "Nothing will work if you don't." To move from 4.0 to 4.5, you'll need to work harder than you ever have before.

Are you prepared to put in the tremendous amount of on-court work needed to take your ball striking to the next level? Can you commit to the off-court training that will get your body in peak condition?

Tennis is a game of movement, and it becomes even more so at the higher levels. Are you willing to drop the five to ten extra pounds you may be carrying so you can have more speed and endurance on the court? These are the questions you need to ask yourself. If the answer is yes, I would suggest the following:

- Find a qualified teaching pro to analyze and improve your mechanics.
- Hire a fitness trainer to design a tennis-specific workout program.
- Speak with a nutritionist so that you're making the best choices in what you eat and drink.

If the answer is no—as it is with most whose lives involve more than tennis—that's OK. You are still a heck of a tennis player. Keep working hard to improve and enjoy the game.

Are You Ready to Play on a USTA Team?

I get it, playing matches and being on a team is fun. Plus, tennis experts stress the need for developing players to get involved in a competitive atmosphere as soon as possible. Competition, we have always been told, allows us to test our skills under pressure and brings out the best in us. All that may be true, however, getting involved in a competitive situation too soon can have disastrous results.

I once had a student, Tom, who was an ex-college basketball player. A great athlete, Tom loved competition and picked up tennis quickly. After a few weeks, he was able to rally back and forth a bit and push his serve in the court most of the time.

One day, Tom told me that he wanted to join his wife's 3.5 USTA team. I gently told him that his game was coming along nicely, but he just wasn't ready for competition.

I went on to explain that, because of his athleticism and competitive drive, he might be able to hang in there in a 3.5-level game but would likely end up playing survival tennis—frantically running around the court, swatting his racket any way possible to get the ball over the net. Tom nodded, said he totally understood, walked away, and promptly signed up for his wife's team.

A week later, Tom and his wife walked to the court for their first match together, holding hands, big smiles on their faces. An hour later, they left the club separately. There was not a smile to be seen, and I suspect the ride home was tougher than their brief match.

I watched that match, and it was ugly! On each point, Tom ran left, he ran right, he ran up, he ran back. He even ran into his wife—more than once.

His strokes were equally out of control. He swung late, he swung too hard, he used the wrong grips, the opposite side of the racket, and often, out of desperation, switched hands. Tom was playing survival tennis and struggling mightily to survive.

If you insist on competing before you've developed the basic skills of the game, you're setting yourself up for failure. How can you expect to be able to do something under pressure before you truly know how to do it?

If you play competitively before you ingrain the mechanics of each stroke, you will develop bad habits. Once that happens, it will be very difficult to unlearn them. Plus, with faulty mechanics, playing the game becomes much more difficult, and the potential for frustration and injury becomes far greater.

As I said, I get it. It's fun to play games and enjoy friendly competition. However, do not let your competitive instincts take over. Play socially and practice the techniques you're working on in your lessons. Forget about winning and losing. Technique first, competition later.

Chapter 35
Getting the Most Out of Lessons

Working with a qualified teaching professional can be a great way to accelerate your progress. However, be sure to choose your teacher wisely. As in any industry, tennis teaching has its pros and pretenders. For every truly qualified professional, there are one or two poseurs who have no business giving lessons. Before giving someone your time and money to teach you tennis, be certain that they:

1. **Have a good reputation.** Every pro has a reputation—good or bad. Be sure to check them out. Speak to your friends, other players, and go online.

2. **Are certified.** The United States Professional Tennis Association (USPTA) and the Professional Tennis Registry (PTR) offer certifications for teaching professionals. Having one (or both) of these certifications is an indication that the person is both qualified and serious about his profession.

3. **Have the proper experience.** The pro you choose should have experience coaching people at your level of play. Some coaches are more experienced with high-performance players, while others specialize in beginners or juniors. Don't be embarrassed to ask.

4. **Are knowledgeable.** The pro should know—and be able to explain clearly—the advantages and disadvantages of the various grips as they relate to every shot in the game. They must be able to look at your game and analyze your strengths and weaknesses technically, tactically, and athletically.

5. **Encourage feedback.** Secure coaches encourage questions and feedback. Insecure ones feel threatened by both. Ask your coach to

honestly assess your level of play and tell you what you need to do to improve. When he tells you something, don't be afraid to ask why. A tennis lesson should be a two-way street. Beware of any instructor that has their own method and doesn't ask for (or seem interested in) your input.

6. **Are punctual and don't waste time during the lesson.** You're paying for a full, high-quality lesson and you should receive it. Beware of the pro who cuts corners by:
   - Coming to the court late
   - Doing an inordinately long warmup
   - Taking extended water or bathroom breaks
   - Giving long-winded explanations
   - Doing too frequent ball pick-ups

These are all tricks of the trade used by lazy pros to cut time off your lesson.

7. **Are engaged.** The lesson should be all about YOU. If the pro begins to tell you about his life or check his cell phone during YOUR time, find another pro.
8. **Are able and willing to adapt.** Some players learn better by hearing, others by seeing. Be sure that the pro is able to tailor his teaching to your style of learning.
9. **Have patience.** Though a struggling student can be frustrating for the instructor, the feeling is much worse for the student. The experienced pro knows this and can not only keep the student's spirits up but help them work through their difficulty. These pros remember how difficult it was for them to learn the game and tell the student stories about how they struggled with the same shot when they first started. It's said that patience is a virtue. For the tennis teaching professional, it is as much a necessity as a racket and basket of balls.
10. **Keep your lessons fresh, interesting, and fun.** Though there is a great deal of repetition required to ingrain the various strategies and techniques of the game, you should not be doing the same drills, the same way, and hearing the same words every lesson. A good pro works hard to plan his lessons. He looks for new drills, uses various teaching

aids, and searches for different ways of expressing his teaching points. A dedicated pro also increases his knowledge and expertise by attending seminars, discussing teaching and playing trends with respected colleagues, and studying tennis books and videos.

11. **Are available even when you're not paying for their time.** Your pro should give you—and encourage you to use—his cell phone number and/or email address. The student/teacher relationship should always extend beyond the court.

Help Them Help You

When you commit to improving your tennis, the first thing you must understand is your learning style. Generally, people learn in one of three ways: through seeing (visual), hearing (auditory) or doing (kinesthetic). To help you determine your style of learning here are a few words on each.

Visual learners absorb information and learn best by seeing. If you're a visual learner, ask your pro to demonstrate the technique you're working on several times. Ask him to show you pictures or video of the technique.

Auditory learners learn best through language. If this is your learning style, ask your pro a lot of questions and encourage feedback and corrections. Tell him to be very specific about what he wants you to learn.

Kinesthetic learners learn by doing. If you're a kinesthetic learner, you'll process and absorb information most effectively by moving, hitting balls and being in match-like situations. You need to know what the various movements feel like. By doing this, repeatedly, you'll develop a frame of reference.

Before wrapping up this chapter, I'd like to address two more issues that frequently come up regarding teaching pros.

1. **Should you take lessons from more than one pro?**

Many players today take lessons from several instructors at one time. Their thinking is that each pro provides a different perspective and feedback. Perhaps one pro will see something another has missed.

The truth is our games are not complicated projects that require a think tank to discover what's needed to get us to the next level. Fundamentals are fundamentals, and high-percentage strategy is high-percentage strategy. There's an old saying:

"A man with two watches never knows what time it is."

Taking lessons from more than one pro frequently accomplishes nothing more than confusion. The pros may have conflicting viewpoints on technique and strategy, or they may want to emphasize different things at different stages. As a result, you'll need to weed through what to take from each coach. It's often a lot of wasted time, energy, and money.

That said, each pro has his own personality and ideas. Some will take a slower, more methodical approach to teaching, while others set a faster pace. Both work and can be fun.

The critical thing is that you're receiving quality, consistent information and have a methodical plan for progress.

It would be ideal if your various pros communicated with each other to make sure everyone is on the same page. Unfortunately, that's not likely to happen. That being the case, it's up to you to take charge of your progress.

If you worked on a Continental grip with John at your private lesson on Monday, be sure Michelle knows that at your group session on Wednesday. Then, she can continue to reinforce the grip during your session. If Michelle introduces serving and volleying to your group, tell John. At your next private lesson, ask to spend some time on serving and volleying.

If you simply move from one pro to another with no communication, you'll likely end up working on a little bit of everything and truly learn nothing!

2. Don't be fooled by the trophies

It's always fun to hear people talk about their tennis instructors because they often gloat about what a great player they are or were:

"Bob played #1 for Florida State in 1977."
"Sam played Wimbledon in 1972."
"Christine had a win over someone who had a win over a player who went three sets with Serena when Serena was 12."

I say to those players, who cares? The fact that Bob, Sam or Christine might have a closet full of trophies, a boat load of newspaper clippings, or a serve the breaks the sound barrier has virtually nothing to do with whether they're qualified to teach you the game.

While a teaching pro certainly needs to have the technical skills to demonstrate various techniques, feed balls at different cadences and speeds, and hit at a level that can push his students, the points previously mentioned are far more important.

Many great players are giving lessons only because they can't play anymore. They act as if teaching is a chore and, unless you're a promising player, have little interest. To the true pro, it doesn't matter if you're a tournament competitor or have difficulty putting one foot in front of another. They're equally eager to see you, help you improve and have a great time doing it.

Your pro should be there for you and everything that he says and does should reflect that. He is not there to regale you with stories of his triumphs nor is he there to blow you off the court.

I've seen teaching pros actually get upset when one of their students hits a winning shot past them. Their fragile ego is bruised so, on the next point, they blast a winner past the poor student to remind them who's the boss.

A true professional's greatest wish is to have one of their students become good enough to beat them. That's their job and if a student becomes better than them, they've done that job well. When one of their players hits a winning shot past them, they cheer like that player has just won Wimbledon. They know how great the student feels having beaten the pro and they feel great for them. It's the student's turn to shine and the good pros know it.

> *You are either a product of your coaching or a victim of your coaching.*
>
> *– Ed Krass*
> **USTA High-Performance Coach**

There are thousands of great teaching professionals out there who had very little success in tournament play. They're great instructors because they can truly empathize with the trials and tribulations of the recreational player.

There are also great players who become fabulous teachers. Mats Wilander immediately comes to mind. The fact is, for the vast majority of those taking lessons, their instructor's tournament record is irrelevant.

Yes, if you are an elite player, it does help to work with a pro who's "been there." Brad Gilbert is an excellent example of this. He's had success on the pro tour and understands what it takes to win at that level. He also has an incredible understanding of the game's strategies and the ability to point out a player's strengths, weaknesses, and patterns.

Would I trust him to teach a complete beginner, with limited athletic ability, who's not sure if they really want to play tennis? Not necessarily.

My message here is that, when you're looking for someone to teach you (or your children), don't be blinded by the light shining off of their trophies.

Do your research and make certain that the person you are considering has the knowledge, communication and emotional skills and, most important, the desire to help you.

Chapter 36
The Camera Doesn't Lie

When I give lessons, one of my favorite sayings is that "the strings don't lie." By this I mean that regardless of what type of backswing, stance, grip, or follow-through you use, the ball will go where your strings are pointing at the moment of impact.

If your shots are going down into the net, that means your strings are facing down. If the ball flies into the sky, your strings are facing up. If it goes to the left…you get the idea. The strings don't lie.

Neither does the camera. One of the best ways to improve your tennis, both technically and tactically, is to video your practice sessions and matches. The truth is most players suffer from a major disconnect between what they think their body is doing and what is actually happening.

Often, my students think they're preparing their racket early when, in fact, their racket doesn't move until the ball has bounced in front of them. They think they've bent their knees to get their racket below the ball, yet their knees are virtually locked. They think they're keeping their head still when they strike the ball when, in fact, they lift their head just before the ball has touched their strings.

This same disconnect exists from a strategic perspective. In post-match discussions, players have sworn to me that they mixed up their serves when they've served to the same spot ninety percent of the time. They tell me they relentlessly attacked the net when, in fact, they came in five times—in three sets.

Videoing your tennis will provide the evidence that will help you bridge that disconnect. Watching your video will give you a dose of reality, and once the initial shock wears off, it will help be a valuable component in your overall plan for improvement.

What You Need

Years ago, recording your tennis was a major endeavor. The camera was massive and cumbersome to operate. Once videoing was done, you popped a VHS cassette out of the camera, inserted it into a player, and then watched the video on a television screen. Today, all you need is a smartphone or tablet. Both have high-quality cameras that give you clear and revealing footage of your game.

To keep the camera secure, mount it on a tripod. You can buy one online for around $25. Place the tripod on a solid surface so that the camera doesn't move around as you play. Stay away from selfie sticks or having a friend hold the camera in his hand—both will likely give you blurry, shaky videos.

How to Video

To video your groundstrokes and volleys, position the camera to the side of your body—90 degrees to your right or left—so that you get a good view of your strokes as well as the split second when your racket strikes the ball. To video your overhead and serve, place the camera behind you. Be sure to position it far enough away so that your entire body and swing (including the follow-through and finish) are captured.

Begin videoing with no ball. Go very slowly and shadow swing each stroke ten times. Without the pressure of moving and having to deal with a ball, you'll be able to record technically proficient strokes. This will help reinforce the brain/body connection. It will also provide you with a baseline from which you can see how well (or poorly) your strokes hold up when you add the ball and, ultimately, movement into the equation.

Next, progress to drop-hitting. Watch the video to see if your strokes remain smooth. Then, using a ball machine, backboard, or practice partner, video yourself hitting on the move.

To video your play, it's best to position the camera behind, and above, the court (looking forward toward the net) so that you can see the action from both sides.

Most tennis courts have an 18–21-foot setback (from the baseline to the fence) with a 10-foot-high fence. If you mount the camera near the top of the fence, you'll have a full view of the entire court. You can purchase excellent fence mounts for your smartphone on the internet for as little as $10.

If you're videoing an official tournament or USTA match, it's good etiquette to get your opponent's permission before you start recording.

Reviewing Your Video

It's best to have someone with a knowledgeable eye review your videos with you. If you work with a teaching professional bring him your video. Better yet, insist that he video—and then review—one of your lessons. He'll be able to pick up and explain the intricacies of your strokes that you'll likely overlook and perhaps also not understand.

If you don't work with a pro, go to your local club and ask to schedule an appointment with one of their pros to review your video. Expect to pay for his time.

As you—or you and your pro—watch the video, be sure to slow it down from time to time. There are certain elements of technique that are impossible to pick up at normal speed. Here are a few important basics to look for when reviewing your videos.

- Do you have a proper ready position? Do you return to it after each shot?
- Do you split step every time before your practice partner strikes the ball?
- Do you immediately turn your hips and shoulders to prepare your racket? Could you do it faster?
- Are you hitting completely through the ball on your groundstrokes?
- Are you keeping your eyes on your point of contact for one recovery step after all your shots?
- Is your service toss consistently accurate?

When you review your matches, look for things such as:

- Your first-serve percentage.
- Service placement. Many players mistakenly serve to the same spot virtually every time.
- Your return of serve percentage.

- The depth of your groundstrokes. Many players will swear that they're hitting to within three feet of the baseline on a consistent basis when the majority of their balls are landing around the service line.

If you play primarily doubles, pay attention to:

- Which team more often wins the race to the net. Remember, the team that controls the net controls the point.
- Your team's aggressiveness. Are you both being active at the net, poaching and faking?
- Your team's movement. Are you moving up and back as well as side to side together? Or is one player breaking down and opening holes in the court?
- How effectively you and your partner communicate with each other.

> *Keep critique of the match factual and not personal. The discussion should revolve around what was or was not done rather than who was to blame.*
>
> **– Stan Smith**
> **Tennis Legend**

Finally, whether you're playing singles or doubles, pay close attention to your own body language and on-court demeanor. Specifically, how do you respond when:

- You hit a winning shot.
- You commit an unforced error.
- You feel your opponent has given you a bad line call.
- You win the match.
- You lose the match.
- Your partner commits an error.
- Your partner makes a technical or tactical suggestion.

Do you like the body language and on-court demeanor you see?

Statistics

For a deeper dive into your game, there are some great software packages available where you can upload your video and have both a technical and tactical analysis done. My three favorites are:

1. Dartfish: Dartfish.com.
2. Tennis Analytics: tennisanalytics.net.
3. Game Smart Tennis: gamesmarttennis.com.

If you really want to take your analysis to the next level, try wearing a wireless microphone during your next practice session or match. Simply clip the microphone to your shirt, a wireless transmitter (which generally weighs less than two ounces) to your shorts, and you're good to go.

If you're working on strokes, you can make comments and give yourself reminders that you can later go back to and review. If you're playing a match, it will be revealing and educational to see how you talk to yourself at various times throughout the match.

An online search will offer a wide variety of wireless microphone systems to choose from starting at around $100. You can also buy a microphone belt that you wear to hold the transmitter.

It may feel a bit awkward at first, but after a few games you'll forget it's there. Again, online you'll find a variety of microphone belts starting at around $25.

How Often to Video

If you're working on a new technique or making a technical change, video yourself twice a week to be sure you're staying on track and practicing the right things.

For match play, video as many matches as possible. Each match will present different scenarios in terms of score, strategies, and interactions between you, your partner, and your opponents. You can learn from them all.

Finally, try not to be too disappointed when you see yourself on video for the first time. We're all used to watching the pros on television (or in person), displaying their smooth strokes and fluid movement. We don't look like that and that's OK. By videoing often—and keeping your videos—you'll build a video library where you can continue to learn as well as enjoy seeing the progress you make.

Chapter 37
How to Climb Out of a Slump

One day, you feel like Federer. You glide around the court, your racket feels like a feather in your hand, and the ball looks as big as a basketball. You're playing great. Then, suddenly, it all disappears.

Your legs feel heavy, every other shot is mishit, and you're losing to players who shouldn't even be on the same court with you. You're officially in a slump. How long you'll stay there will be up to you.

Slumps can have physical or mental causes. Here are a few examples of each.

Physical

- Dealing with an injury. Trying to play through a nagging injury can cause you to struggle to properly execute your strokes.
- You're making some type of technical change. For example, learning a new grip, trying a different string tension, or using a new racket. Initially, changes like these can cause your level of play to drop.
- Playing too much. If you're playing too often, you may tire or even suffer an injury.
- Playing too little. You may not be hitting enough balls to maintain your level.

Mental

- You can become burned out from playing too much tennis.
- Becoming too concerned about wins or losses.

- Your negative and judgmental inner voice becomes overwhelming.
- Off-court problems can interfere with your play.

The next time you find yourself in a slump, here are a few tips to help you get beyond it.

- **Accept that slumps happen to all players.** Even the pros fall into slumps from time to time. Remind yourself of this. Take comfort in the fact that you're not alone, and you will eventually come out of it. Everyone does.
- **Maintain a positive attitude during your practice and matches.** Easier said than done, but your inner voice has a tremendous impact on your mental state and performance. Become aware of when negative and judgmental thoughts begin to creep in.
- **Forget about the results.** Again, easier said than done, but by detaching yourself from winning and losing, you'll relieve a lot of the pressure and your play will improve. Instead of the score, focus on playing high-percentage tennis and striking each ball solidly.
- **Set different goals.** Instead of making your matches all about winning or losing, set other goals. For example, getting seventy percent of your first serves in, preparing your racket as quickly as possible, or attacking the net at every opportunity.
- **Take some lessons.** Working with a qualified teaching professional is a great way to reset your game.
- **Mix it up.** Play with different players at other venues. Take a hiatus from your USTA matches and play some social games. You can even schedule some fun matches with players a level or two below you. When you play with weaker players, there'll be no pressure, they'll greatly appreciate it, and you can focus on what tennis should be—fun.
- **Take a break.** If you're playing multiple days each week or playing on several teams, you might just be tired of tennis. A short break can relax your mind, rest your body, and re-energize your passion for the game.

My Truth

Many tennis teachers dream of developing the next Roger Federer or Serena Williams. I couldn't care less about that. My passion has always been working with recreational players.

To me, success has nothing to do with wins, rankings, or ratings. Those all come and go and often have little to do with how well or poorly a person played.

My goal in writing this book was to provide you with both clarity and perspective. Clarity in terms of the key elements of tennis which will help you become a better player. As I said in my Introduction, there are no secrets or shortcuts. There are only time-tested facts, fundamentals, and hard work. If you commit to the instruction offered in this book, your tennis will improve. I guarantee it.

However, it won't happen immediately. This is where perspective enters the picture. First, perspective in terms of your game. If you practice frequently, and properly, you'll improve. If you don't you won't. It's that simple.

Finally, and most important, maintain perspective in terms of tennis' place in your life. Playing tennis should make you happy. Even if you don't play as well as you once did or hoped to, never put down your racket. The game has so much to offer.

Tennis provides a fantastic full-body workout. It's a strategic activity that engages your brain and releases feel-good hormones (endorphins) which can improve your mental health, reduce stress, and lower your risk of depression.

Plus, there's always something to work on and improve. I recently gave a series of lessons to a wonderful lady named Ruth who wanted more power on her groundstrokes. Ruth is 94 years old!

She and her husband Al, 95, come to my club every summer. They play four days a week and celebrated their 70th anniversary on our courts. Al is now no longer able to play but Ruth stills takes lessons and hits off the backboard.

Another player, Jack, is 83 years old and came to me to prepare for senior tournaments. As I was warming him up for his first match, Jack confessed to me how "incredibly nervous" he was. I told him that I thought that was wonderful. *To be 83 and still engaged in something to the point it made him nervous was fantastic,* I thought.

Finally, playing tennis is just fun. This point was driven home to me a few years ago. Katie, Claire, Maria and Jean were coming to me for a weekly lesson. After, they'd go out to dinner and drinks. They didn't practice in between lessons and didn't improve a bit during the time we'd played together.

Though it was a bit frustrating for me as their pro, Katie said something that gave me tremendous perspective. At the end of a point, I made a comment regarding a shot Katie hit. I said, "Katie, that's a nice shot today but at the next level you'll need to…" Katie smiled and said, "Greg, what's wrong with this level?" The answer, of course, was "nothing."

I teach tennis, and wrote *The Truth About Tennis*, to help players like Ruth, Jack and Katie achieve their goals. Whether it's to become a highly rated USTA competitor or simply play tennis with your friends before a night out, I hope that tennis is an enjoyable part of your life for the rest of your life.

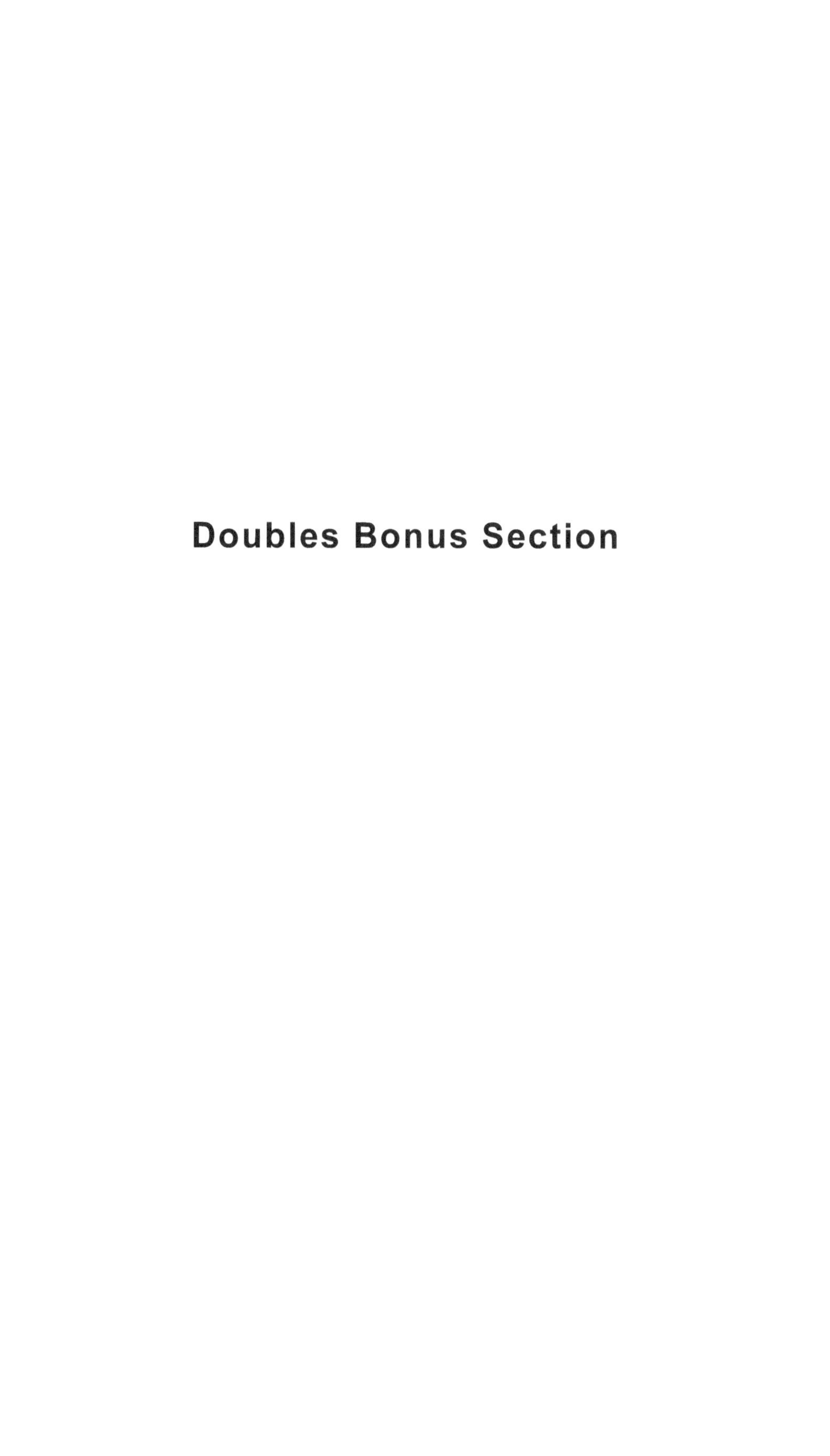

Doubles Bonus Section

Why Everyone Should Play Doubles

I love doubles. I love to play it, watch it, teach it, and study it. Most recreational players clearly agree as each day millions of people of all ages, sizes, and athletic ability step onto the doubles court. That's why I'm adding this bonus section to my book.

The truth is anyone who is serious about becoming a complete player should spend time playing doubles. Even dedicated singles players—and especially juniors—will see their game dramatically improve if they play some doubles. Here are just a few of the benefits the game offers.

- **Your game will become more versatile.** Doubles forces you to execute a wide variety of shots to be successful. You'll need to be able to hit volleys, half volleys, drop volleys, reflex volleys, slice, overheads, and lobs. This is especially important for developing juniors who tend to plant themselves behind the baseline and hit only groundstrokes.

- **Your shots will become more precise.** With two players across the net, you can't simply float the ball back in play. You'll have to learn to vary the height, pace, and spin of your shots—especially your serve and return of serve.

- **You'll become quicker.** With four players on the court, points will be fast paced, forcing you to develop better anticipation skills, quicker reflexes, and court awareness.

- **Your footwork and balance will improve.** If you play primarily singles, most of your movement tends to be side to side. Doubles forces you to not only move side to side but forward and back, bend and stretch, as well as gain and regain your balance—several times every point.

- **You'll develop a better understanding of strategy**. Many singles players take the court and blast away or push every ball back over the net. They give little, if any, thought to what they're trying to do or how each shot fits into the construction of a point. Doubles is more three-dimensional. With two opponents, you'll be forced to use the entire court and learn how to create openings. You and your partner will have to discuss strategy and tactics before, during, and after your matches.

- **Your people skills will improve**. Both you and your partner will screw up from time to time. You'll learn that being supportive and encouraging will bring far more positive results than negative comments and body language. Once you realize that your partner plays better with this approach, you might try the same thing on yourself and see how your own game improves.

In the pages that follow, I'll go over some of the key elements of doubles. However, first you need to master…

The Seven Volleys

To win doubles matches at the 4.0 level and above, you and your partner must be able to volley well. If you can't, you'll likely have to resort to playing from the one-up, one-back formation, which will make it much more difficult to beat high-level teams.

To be a force at the net, you need to become comfortable hitting the following seven volleys.

1. **Routine volley.** When you watch recreational players practice their volleys, this is the one you see them hitting the most. The ball is in a comfortable strike zone (shoulder height), and it's an easy volley to move forward and attack with a short, slightly downward motion. Most players excel at the routine volley. Unfortunately, at the higher levels, your opponents will seldom give you routine volleys.

2. **Stretch volley.** When you're forced to reach or stretch for the ball, you'll be off-balance. This can cause your arm and wrist to become loose and floppy, leading to a loss of control. When stretching for a volley, focus on keeping your arm and wrist firm.

3. **Low volley.** If you're playing doubles at the 4.0 level and above, I guarantee you'll be hitting a lot of low volleys. To handle them effectively, bend your knees to lower your center of gravity and slightly open your racket face. The truth is if you're not using the Continental grip—which naturally opens your racket face—you're going to struggle with balls hit below the net.

4. **Tweener.** Arguably the most missed volley, the "tweener" is too high for a routine volley and too low to hit as an overhead. Players often commit to hitting an overhead, suddenly realize they can't swing fast enough, and end up hitting the ball into the back fence. The best way

to play the tweener is to move forward (attacking it with your feet) and simply volley it back in play.

5. **Block volley.** The next time you're faced with a fast-moving ball coming right at you, put your racket in front of your body, squeeze your grip a bit tighter and let the ball hit the strings. Your opponent has provided the power, so you simply focus on solid contact.

6. **Drop volley.** Is best hit when you're within 10 feet of the net and the ball is between your shoulders and knees. Think of it as an exaggerated slice where you bring your racket from a high-to-low position. At contact, loosen your grip and scoop under the ball. This will soften the shot as well as add a bit of backspin.

7. **Lob volley.** Four players are at the net, exchanging fast-paced volleys, each team trying to inch closer so they can finish the point. In this intense net duel, if you or your partner can execute a well-placed lob volley, you'll likely get your opponent's scrambling.

To hit a lob volley, loosen your grip and open your racket face slightly (strings toward the sky) just before contact. Focus on hitting under the ball. This will allow you to push the ball up off your racket and over your opponents' heads.

Though it can be a devastating weapon, the lob volley is a risky shot because, with four players up close, if you don't get the ball up high enough, you've given your opponents an easy overhead with two very inviting targets—you and your partner!

And then there's the swinging volley

I didn't include this increasingly popular volley in my list of must-haves for one reason. I can't stand it! I feel it's a reckless, impatient shot that requires superb timing and has a huge potential for error.

You'll see players try a swinging volley when they're stuck in no-man's-land or moving to the net. They take a massive swing, often jumping off the ground and letting out a primal scream as they strike the ball. It all looks and sounds very impressive and can be intimidating—on those rare occasions they hit the ball into the court. For most players, the risk is simply not worth the reward.

Instead, when faced with a floating ball in the mid court, move forward, hit a traditional approach volley, and continue to the net. You can then look to end the point with a higher-percentage volley or overhead.

Does It Really Matter Who
You Play With?

In a perfect world, you have a set partner. You play matches together, practice as a team, and take lessons together. Well, we all know it's not a perfect world, and finding a regular partner doesn't always happen. The good news is that having a consistent partner, though ideal, is overrated. What's far more important is that you team up with a person who's receiving the same instruction as you.

Some coaches teach an aggressive approach to strategy, advocating players take the ball early and try to end the point in less than three shots. Other coaches (like me) favor a more disciplined, high-percentage game plan. Therefore, it's imperative that you and your partner walk onto the court with a similar perspective.

I like to say that a player from my 9:00 a.m. class on Monday can partner with a player they've never met from my 10:00 a.m. class on Friday and they can play well together. They can do this because they've received the same instruction. The most important element of that is the role of each player. The following pages contain that instruction.

The Serving Team

When you're serving, you have three goals:

1. Get a high percentage of first serves in.
2. Put your opponent off-balance.
3. Follow your serve to the net.

When you get a high percentage (70% or more) of first serves in play, the receiver won't know what to expect in terms of placement, spin, or speed. He'll have to react quickly and hope to hit a reasonable return. When you miss your first serve, you've forfeited that advantage. The receiver knows your second serve is weaker and he'll shift into attack mode.

To be successful, focus on spin and placement, remembering that seventy-five percent of your serves should be hit into the receiver's body and to the T. Here's why:

- The body serve will jam him. This makes it difficult for him to extend his arms and hit an aggressive return.
- Both serves make it difficult for him to return down the line, past your partner at the net.
- Both reduce the angles he has at his disposal.
- Both serves make it easier for your partner to poach.

Keep in mind that playing the percentages entails strategies that assume all other things are equal. However, if you notice that your opponent's backhand is significantly weaker than his forehand, factor that into your serving strategy. You might decide to consistently serve to his weak backhand, or you could serve down the middle more often and wait for a big point to serve to his weaker side.

Follow your Serve to the Net

After you've hit your serve and are on your way forward, you'll have time for approximately three to four running steps. At that point, your opponent is about to hit his return.

Take a strong split step, see where the return is going, and then go get it. Try to be on or inside the service line when you hit your first volley. Notice I said "first" volley.

Very rarely will your opponent's return of serve be a point ending opportunity. Think of it as an approach shot. Return the ball back deep to the receiver, join your partner at the net and begin your movement and anticipation strategies. Yes, if the return of serve is short and high, you may be able to move in and end the point, but don't plan on it.

Should you come in behind your second serve? It depends: if your serve resembles a slow-moving balloon, against a strong player, no. Stay back and move in on a subsequent shot. Against a weak player, charging forward may intimidate them. The bottom line is, if it's working, do it. However, be aware of when it stops working. I promise it will.

Your goal should be to develop strong first and second serves that will allow you to always move forward. Until then, the higher-percentage strategy will likely be to serve, stay back, and try to work your way into the net.

If you don't put the time into developing a serve that you can confidently come in behind, you're basically putting up for grabs two to three games a set that should be heavily weighted in your favor. If your partner also has a weak serve, your team is really going to struggle against opponents at the 4.0 level and above.

Being able to hit effective serves that allow you to join your partner at the net, as well as run various plays, will give your team a huge advantage against all opponents.

When your partner is serving your job is to:

1. Distract the receiver.
2. Pick off as many balls as possible.
3. Follow the ball as it moves back and forth.

When your partner is serving, never forget that you are as responsible for the outcome of the game as he is. In fact, with the right approach, you can control the game without ever touching the ball.

Where to Stand

Start in the exact middle of the service box. Then, depending upon where your partner serves, adjust your position accordingly. If he serves out wide, follow the ball out wide. If the serve goes down the middle, take a step toward the center and look to poach. You and your partner should coordinate this before the point begins.

As the match goes on, pay attention to each receiver's strengths, weaknesses, and tendencies. If one receiver never returns down your alley (maybe, he can't) move more toward the center. If the other never lobs, move in a few feet. If he always lobs, drop back a bit. Stay away from these two common errors:

1. **Lining up too close to the sideline.** The thought here is to protect the alley, but this approach does more harm than good. First, it shows the receiver a big space down the center of the court which will help him relax on his return. It also makes it virtually impossible for you to poach. Yes, if your opponent constantly tries to go down your alley, line up closer to the sideline for a point or two and then move right back to the center of the service box. Constantly adjust.
2. **Lining up too close to the net.** If one opponent never lobs his return of serve, great. Stay up close and look to pick off volleys. However, an alert player will eventually notice that you're too close and start going over your head. When he does, adjust by taking a few steps back.

Crawl Inside Their Heads

When your partner is serving, your job is to create chaos and confusion among your opponents. Get in the receiver's face. Move, fake, and poach. Take the attitude that every ball they hit is yours.

Watch the receiver's body language and racket face. If he's moving forward and his racket is at the same height as the ball, he's probably going to drive his return. Immediately take two steps forward, move diagonally toward the center and try to pick off the shot.

If he's leaning back, his racket drops below the height of the ball, and the racket face opens up, he's going to lob. Quickly take three steps back and get ready to hit an overhead.

Once you get a feel for whether the return is going to be a lob or drive, your next thought is "This shot is mine." Don't be surprised when the ball comes to you. Be surprised when you can't hit it.

Your top priority is to make the receiving team aware, no, make that afraid of you. Doing this will push them into panic mode, which will result in many, many errors.

The Receiving Team

When you're receiving serve, keep these four tactical goals in mind:

1. Return the serve.
2. Keep your return away from the server's partner.
3. If the server moves to the net, aim down at his feet.
4. If the server stays back, return the serve crosscourt, deep, and move to the net.

Above all, do not try to end the point with your return!

As you begin your matches, line up a foot behind the baseline. If you know in advance—or notice during the match—that your opponent has a strong serve, back up accordingly.

In terms of how far laterally you should be positioned, take your cues from the server. An experienced server will vary his position along the baseline. You should too. If they move more toward the center of their court, move toward yours. If he moves out wide, slide over to cut off the likely angle.

As the match progresses, pay attention to the server's strengths and tendencies and adjust your position (up, back, left, right) accordingly. Many players serve to the same spot every single time, while others will give you a clue as to where they're serving by how they stand or where they toss the ball.

For example, if the toss is to the left of the server's body, move to your left. If he tosses the ball wide to his right side, indicating a slice serve, move to your right.

Sometimes, you may be able to pick up a 'tell' from the server. When Boris Becker prepared to serve, for example, Andre Agassi noticed that the German would stick out his tongue in the direction he planned to serve. "The hardest part was not returning his serve," Agassi said. "The hardest part was not letting him know that I knew this."

As you wait for the serve, have a plan for how you're going to return the ball. If you're facing a serve-and-volley opponent, plan on returning the ball low at their feet and then moving forward. If your opponent serves and stays back, aim two to three feet above the net, return crosscourt, deep, and then get to the net as soon as you can.

Just before the serve is struck, take a strong split step, determine which direction the ball is coming, and immediately turn your shoulders and pivot your feet toward the oncoming ball. This quick shoulder turn will prepare your racket.

Once you've determined—using your triple vision—if the server is coming to the net or staying back, hit your return from these options:

1. **Block it.** This is the best approach against a big serve. Using a short shoulder turn, keep your racket out in front of your body and point your strings toward your target. If the server is coming to the net, use a two-shot combination: Block the ball down low, forcing the server to volley up. You or your partner can then move forward and attack. A variation of this would be the chip and charge return. With this strategy, you'll hit a soft slice to the server's feet and then sprint forward, trying to beat him to the net. While moving into the shot, swing down along the backside of the ball, adding slice to your shot. Try to make the ball bounce in front of the server. When the ball bounces, it will stay very low, forcing him to hit up. It's a great play but requires a lot of touch, particularly against a strong serve. If the server is staying back, open your racket face a bit and block the ball back deep.

2. **Drive it.** If you're returning a serve that you feel you can execute a full groundstroke, go for it. However, don't be reckless and try to end the point with your return. When you execute your shoulder turn, turn farther, as you would for a groundstroke. If the server is coming in, step forward, rotate your shoulders, and drive the ball at his feet. If he stays back, aim a bit higher, roll the ball deep, and join your partner at the net.

3. **Lob it.** A well-executed lob return of serve will immediately give your team the advantage. Using the same, short backswing you would for

your block or chip returns, open the racket face a bit more on contact and push the ball over the server's partner. Then, move forward.

As your skills improve and you face opponents at the 4.0 level and above, you'll need to take your tactics to the next level. As the serving team sets up a play before the point begins, the receiving team should as well. Before the point begins, let your partner know where you're going to hit your return: crosscourt, down the alley, right at the net man, or deep with a lob. This communication helps your team in two important ways:

1. Your partner can position himself accordingly. For example, if he knows that you'll be returning at the net man, after the serve is truck, he can quickly shift toward the center of the court. If the volley is high, he can then move forward and attack.
2. By deciding where you're going to hit your return beforehand, you'll take away that brief moment of indecision and be able to focus on hitting a solid ball toward your target.

Take the Server's Partner Out of the Point

When receiving serve against a high-level team you'll undoubtedly have to deal with an active net player. He'll be poaching, faking (which we'll get into soon), and trying to distract you. Here are the three best ways to calm him down:

1. **Hit the occasional shot down his alley**. Do this early in a match. Even if you lose the point, it's worth it. You've planted the seed that you might hit there, making him more hesitant to poach.
2. **Drive your return right at him.** Again, this will keep him on his toes and less eager to poach.
3. **Lob over his head**. This will force him to adjust his starting position, making it more difficult to poach.

By keeping the opposing net player guessing on your return of serve, he'll always have that moment of indecision, and as a result, be less aggressive.

When your partner's receiving serve, be sure to:

1. Keep your eyes fixed on the opposite net player.
2. Notice if the server comes in or stays back.
3. Determine what type of return your partner has hit.

When your partner's returning serve, you're either going to love it or hate it. If he does his job and hits an effective return, you'll be able to move forward, pick off your opponent's shots, and be a hero. But if your partner hits weak returns that your opponents can attack, you'll be a target.

A feast or famine position to say the least, however, with the right strategy you can turn this hot spot into an advantage for your team.

Where to Stand

At the start of each point, you have basically three choices:

1. On the service line
2. 1–2 feet in front of the service line
3. At the baseline

If you're not familiar with your opponent, begin the match on the service line. As you develop a feel for the quality of your opponent's serves and see how well (or poorly) your partner is returning, you can make adjustments.

If the serve is weak, the opposing net player is inactive, or your partner is having a great day returning, move a foot or two in front of the service line. This will put pressure on your opponent because you're now in a better position to move forward after the return.

On those days when your partner is struggling with his service return, or you're facing a great serve, move back to the baseline on your opponent's first serve. Yes, you're conceding the race to the net, but you'll give your team a better chance of staying in the point after a weak return. If the first serve is missed, you can then move back to the service line or even closer to the net. Presumably, your partner will hit a strong return off the second serve, and you can then begin to think offensively.

At the 4.0 level and above, you'll often be facing a strong serve-and-volley player as well as his active partner at the net. As your partner prepares to return serve, stand at a slight angle so that you're facing the server's partner. He's the immediate threat. By standing at this angle, you'll be able to watch and react to his movements much more quickly.

Make a Quick Assessment

Once you hear your partner strike his return, you need to quickly determine what type of shot he's hit and assess the situation. This is **not** done by turning and watching your partner strike the ball.

When you turn your head, you lose sight of what the serving team is doing. If the net player decides to poach, by the time you get your head turned back around, it'll be too late to do anything other than protect yourself.

Initially, focus on the player serving. As soon as he strikes the ball, shift to his partner. Look in his eyes, read his body language, and you'll have all the information you'll need.

You'll be amazed at how the small bit of time gained by watching the server's partner (instead of your own) will allow you to prepare and return balls that, in the past, you've only been able to protect yourself from.

When your partner returns serve, there are five common scenarios:

1.   A weak return that the server or his partner is going to attack

Pay attention to the net player's eyes and body language. If you see his eyes widen and he quickly starts moving across the court, he's poaching. Get your hands up, take a quick step back, execute a strong split step, and do the best you can to react to the hard volley that will soon be coming your way.

If the ball moves past him high, immediately look toward the server. If he's moving forward with wide eyes, again prepare to react quickly because he's probably going to drive his shot right at you.

2.   A strong, low, return net rushing server

When the server's partner remains still, and the ball moves low past him, it's your turn to get excited. If the server is moving forward, the low return will force him to volley up. Look to poach. From this difficult position, the odds of him volleying down your alley are slim. To do so, he must first dig the ball up off the court, change its direction, and then hit it over the highest part of the net. All of these tell you that he's probably going to volley back to your partner. Just before he makes contact, move across the court on a diagonal, pick off his volley, and drive an aggressive shot down the middle.

3.   A deep return to the server who has stayed back

If your partner has hit a deep crosscourt return, and the server has not moved to the net, shift into attack mode. Follow the ball forward and look to be aggressive.

4.   A return at the opposing net player

When your partner returns the serve low to the opposing net player, immediately start moving diagonally toward him. Because the ball is low, he must hit up. When that happens, you'll be there to pick it off. Plus, if he feels you coming at him, it will make an awkward shot even more difficult.

If the return of serve is high, and you see your opponent move forward, he's probably going to hit an aggressive volley between you and your partner. Quickly move to the center of the court.

When you see the net player preparing to hit an overhead, quickly move back. Just before the ball is struck, take a strong split step to balance yourself. Many players feel that they need to get back as far as they can to reply to an oncoming overhead. As a result, they're often caught still backing up as the ball is struck.

When that happens, they're totally off-balance and faced with a powerful overhead coming right at them. You're much better off being a bit closer but balanced. From this position, you'll best be able to react to the shot, and if necessary, protect yourself.

With a weak return that makes you feel physically threatened, abandon ship. Take a crossover step, turn your back and move toward your alley. Give him the big hole down the center. Don't try to be a hero. Concede the point.

5. A lob

If your partner lobs his return over the net player, and both opponents are scrambling back to chase the ball, be careful. You'll see your opponents in trouble and your instincts will undoubtedly urge you and your partner to charge the net. Not so fast!

When in trouble, educated players know that their best option is to hit a high defensive lob. If you and your partner are both charging the net, you might get caught watching the ball sail over your head.

Instead, when you see your opponents' scrambling back for a lob, both you and your partner should position yourselves on or just behind the service line. Then, when the likely lob comes, you're ready for it. If it's short, you can easily move forward to play the ball. Yes, from the service line position you're vulnerable to a low drive, but if both opponents are struggling to get to the ball, that shot is extremely unlikely.

Doubles Dilemmas and Decisions

Doubles means "two" and anytime two people are involved, the potential for confusion arises. Here are a few strategies for three of the game's more confounding dilemmas.

1. Who plays the deuce court and who plays the ad court?

A while back, I read a book on doubles by a much-loved tennis champion. Truly one of the game's all-time greats, the author regaled us with his stories of winning Grand Slam titles and the Davis Cup while at the same time explaining in great detail all of the intricacies that he and his partner considered when deciding who would play which half of the court.

After I finished reading and translating his profound theories, I felt as if I'd swum from Wimbledon to the U.S. Open and back again. I was exhausted, and immediately thought that it can't be this complicated. Fortunately, for most teams, it isn't. Here's the key:

Each player should play the side where he is most comfortable returning serve.

Initially, nothing else matters. If your team doesn't return your opponent's serves effectively, points are going to end quickly. With that in mind, consider the following:

- At the 3.5 level and below, most serves are hit to the outsides of the service boxes.
- At the 4.0 level and above, most serves are hit down the middle of the service box and to the T.

This means that a 3.5-and-below-level team of two right-handed players would want the player with the stronger forehand returning serve from the deuce court and the player with the better backhand returning from the ad court.

Right-handed teams at the 4.0 level and above will be facing primarily serves coming down the middle and the T, so they would want the player who prefers backhands on the deuce side and the player with the better forehand receiving from the ad court.

Since most of the big points (15-30, 30-15, 30-40, 40-30) occur on the ad side, some think the team should have its stronger player there. This makes sense except for the fact that if you can't win points from the deuce side, you may never get to the big points.

So again, it boils down to having each player on the side where they are most comfortable receiving serve. Initially, go with this premise and build from there. Once you make your decision, remember, it's only set in stone for one set. If you feel it's not working, make a change.

Final thought: If you're one of those players who **must** play on a particular side of the court, you're seriously limiting the pool of partners from which you can choose. Spend some time playing on the other side and I think you'll find that you can become equally comfortable. Plus, by playing both sides, you'll gain a broader perspective of the court as well as add to your arsenal of shots. Most of all, it allows you to be flexible, and if you can become comfortable on both sides of the court, you'll have that many more people to team up with.

2. Who Serves First?

A basketball team puts its strongest lineup on the floor at the start of the game and so should you. This means that the player who has the best chance of winning his service game should serve first. Usually, this is the player with the stronger serve that will force weak returns. Not always, though.

I once had a partner, Tony, who had a great serve (much better than mine) but was so active and intimidating at the net that we decided it would be better if I served first. I simply spun my serve in and watched Tony drive our opponents crazy. With his poaching, faking, and great speed, he was able to totally control the point. By putting our best lineup (me serving, Tony at the net) into the game first, so to speak, we were able to set an intimidating tone right from the start of the match.

Look at both factors—who has the stronger serve and who is more active at the net—and go from there. Keep in mind that the person serving first will likely get more opportunities to serve during the set, so make sure your starting lineup is a good one.

Finally, if you or your partner are left-handed, play close attention to the position of the sun. Quite often, you can arrange your serving order so that neither of you will have to serve looking into the sun.

3. Whose Ball Is It?

Singles is easy—any ball that crosses the net is yours. Most of the time in doubles it's also obvious which player should hit the ball. However, there are two situations when there is often confusion—balls hit down the center of the court and shots lobbed over your heads.

In both cases, one of two things usually happens: Either both players go for the ball and run into each other, or much more common, they turn and give each other a "Where were you?" look as the ball flies between them.

Who Covers the Middle?

It's not as confusing as you think. When you and your partner are both at the net, you should be moving from side to side, following the ball. If the ball goes to your opponent's deuce court, you and your partner should move to your left. In this situation, the player playing the deuce court takes shots hit down-the-middle. Yes, it's likely that player's backhand weaker volley, however, in a fast-paced game, he should cover the middle.

An exception to this would be if the return down the middle is a high, slow-moving ball. In that case, it's a perfect opportunity for the player covering the alley to call "Mine", explode toward the middle, cut off the return, and volley the ball with his stronger forehand.

If the ball is hit to your opponent's ad court, you and your partner will both shift to the right. Your team's ad-court player then covers the middle.

The only time there may be some confusion with these general guidelines is when your team returns the ball right down the center of the court. In that situation, you both should take a step toward the center. If your opponent then returns your shot down the middle, the player closer to the net should take it. If you and your partner are both at the net, the player with the stronger shot (usually the forehand) should take it.

Who covers the Lobs?

"Yours" is often the cry among recreational players when they see a lob go up. They turn, look at their partners, who stare right back at them as the ball floats over their heads. To play the net effectively, you and your partner must iron out who's going to cover which lob because one of the first things a smart team will do is test you with lobs.

Let's say that Joe and Trevor are at the net and the lob goes over Joe's head. Now what? There are two schools of thought. The first says that Trevor should go for the ball because it's more comfortable for him to move across the court at an angle than it would be for Joe to move back for a ball that's directly over his head.

This is a perfectly workable strategy for players at the 3.0 level and below who haven't yet developed their movement skills. The duck and switch strategy allows the team to cover the lob and get the ball back in play.

The problem with this is that Trevor, having to cross the court to run behind Joe, will be running a longer distance than Joe would to reach the lob. He'll also likely have to let the ball bounce and give up control of the net. Finally, it puts their team in the vulnerable one-up, one-back formation.

Certainly, there will be situations where covering your own lob is impossible however, the more advanced approach says that, if at all possible, each player should cover his own lobs. When a lob goes over Joe's head, if his anticipation and movement skills are developed, he'll be able to move back and play the shot. His first choice would be to hit the lob as an overhead smash. If he can't get balanced to hit the overhead, he should still take the ball out of the air but simply volley the ball back deep into the opponent's backcourt. This allows him and Trevor to still maintain control of the net.

Whether its returning balls hit down the middle of the court or lobs hit over your heads, if there's ever doubt as to who should hit the ball, go after it yourself. Most likely, the worst that will happen is that you and your partner will bang rackets. It's much better to have two players going after a ball than none. After all, it doesn't matter who **should have** hit the ball, you both lose the point if no one goes for it.

Elements of Communication

Whether you have a regular partner or are playing with someone for the first time, it's essential that you agree on how you'll communicate with each other. Communication between you and your partner has four elements.

1. When you first decide to team up.

Before you and your new partner begin competing, decide how to share your thoughts before, during, and after your matches. For example, ask each other:

- What would you like me to say to you after you miss an easy shot?
- What can I do during our matches to help you stay positive and focused?
- Do you want to hear advice from me during our matches?
- After we lose a match, how long should we wait to talk about it?

2. Pre-match.

Discuss your opponents. If you've faced them before, go over their strengths, weaknesses, and tendencies as well as your team's strategy. For example:

- Each time Tony served to you on game point, he served out wide.
- Claire's second serve is really weak so, when she misses her first serve, remember to attack her second.
- Mike hasn't hit a lob since 2010, so when we move forward, we can position ourselves on top of the net.
- If I start to miss my first serve, remind me to keep my head up.

- Make sure you're not too aggressive on your first volley. Hit it back cross-court, and then we can settle in at the net.
- We've got to remember to lob when we're in trouble.

If you're facing the team for the first time and don't know anyone who has played them, begin the match playing high-percentage tennis. As the match progresses, continue to analyze and discuss potential changes in strategy that might become necessary.

3. During the Match

When the ball is in play, obviously, there can be no extended conversations. However, there will often be situations when a quick, single word of direction is necessary. For example, when your team is at the net and your opponent throws up a lob, one of you should quickly say "Mine." If you know you have no chance at the ball, say "Yours."

If you're running down a lob that's gone over your partner's head, a quick "Switch" will remind them to move to the other side if they haven't already. If you're really struggling to chase down the lob and are certain you'll hit a weak shot, yell "Back" to bring him to the baseline with you. Lastly, if your opponent's lob looks like it's going out, the player not going after the ball should shout, "Bounce it." That will prevent the player from hitting a ball that lands outside the lines.

Always Keep It Positive

Doubles points can be extremely intense and strenuous, so when the point ends, you and your partner need to keep each other pumped up and focused on the match. If your partner double faulted three times in a row, use this time to help him regain his confidence. If you notice something your opponents are, or are not, doing strategically you can make adjustments.

Keep the conversation simple, positive, and above all, non-judgmental. Here's my top ten list of things to **never** say to your partner before, during or after a match.

10. We have to win this one.

9. How could you miss that shot?

8. I could have had that.

7. Stay on your side.

6. That's the third overhead in a row you hit into the bottom of the net.

5. I can't believe we're losing to these guys.

4. You really stink today.

3. See if you can hold your serve this time.

2. I never lost to this team with my last partner.

And my all-time favorite:

1. We're losing because of you.

Believe it or not, I've heard players spit out every one of these to their partners during matches. Aside from being extremely obnoxious, these comments do your partner and team no good whatsoever.

Be Aware of Body Language

The shoulder slump, rolling of the eyes, dropped head, and the hands-on-the-hips stance are just a few of the more common reactions insensitive doubles players use to express their displeasure over an unforced error by their partner.

Nobody tries to miss a shot or blow a point. Negative body language can cut like a knife and take your partner completely off his game. Plus, when your opponents see this, they'll know there's dissension on your team, and that will only pump them up.

Every tennis player in the world has bad days from time to time. A good partner knows this and understands that his teammate was not planning to double fault twice each service game or volley into the net on break point. Rather than beat him down further, an experienced partner will do things to pick up his struggling teammate.

The next time your partner makes one of those horrible, unforced errors at a big moment, use positive body language: Stand tall and pick up your shoulders. Walk up to him, pat him on the back and say positive things like:

- Don't sweat it, we'll get this one.
- No problem. Let's keep being aggressive.

- Come on. We can still come back and win this match.

Even though your partner may be playing the worst tennis of his life, using words like "we" and "let's" will show him that you're a resilient team no matter what.

The Changeover

Review the previous two games and analyze how your team is winning and losing points. If your opponents are beating you to the net, figure out a strategy to keep them back. If you notice that one of your opponents has a weak overhead, commit to lobbing him.

During this time, sneak a glance at the other team. Check out their body language. Do they appear tired, frustrated, or angry? If they're arguing, it means you're getting to them so stick with the game plan you've been using.

4. After the Match

Discuss the match as soon as possible while things are still fresh in your mind. Do a team analysis of the match from a technical, strategic, emotional, and physical perspective.

Technically, look at how your shots held up during the pressure of the match. Ask each other questions, such as:

- Were we both able to get a high percentage of first serves in?
- How well did we return serve?
- Were our volleys consistent and penetrating?
- How about overheads? Were we both solid when lobbed?
- Was the slice backhand return of serve he's been working on effective?

Strategically, look at things such as:

- Were we able to force our opponents to play our game, or did they dictate the match?
- Did the serve-and-volley strategy work well for our team?

- Were we able to execute at least one successful poach in each service game?
- What adjustments did we make after we lost the first set?
- Are we getting more comfortable with both of us at the net?

Emotionally, ask yourselves:

- Were we able to keep our emotions in check, or did we let adversity get to us?
- When we got down a break, were we able to pick each other up and stage a comeback, or did we collapse?
- When the big points arrived, how did we respond? Did we rise to the occasion, or did we choke?

If nerves got the better of you, you need to recreate that pressure when you play your practice matches. A great way to simulate match pressure is to grab another team, take to the practice court, and play practice sets from specific scoring situations. Here are two of my favorites:

1. Play a set where each player gets only one serve and each game begins at 30-40. Having to hit a second serve on break point is one of the greatest pressures you'll face during your matches.

2. Play a set where the team that wins each game gets a point advantage in the next game. If your team is serving and wins the first game, your opponents serve the second down 0-15. If you win that game, your partner then serves the third game with a lead of 30-0. If your opponents fight back and win that game, they then serve with a lead of 15-0. It's a great exercise that will teach your team how to play both when you're ahead and behind.

Physically, ask each other:

- Were we both able to get to the net as quickly in the third set as we did in the first?
- Did our overheads hold up as well in the third set as the first?
- Did our shoulders tire in the third set? How about our legs?

Keep in mind that even the slightest physical decline can affect your team's performance. If fatigue causes you to be a step slower getting to the net or moving back for an overhead, it can make the difference between hitting an effective shot or committing an error.

You may have the best strokes at the club, but if you don't have the energy to get to the ball or the strength to swing the racket, your beautiful strokes become useless. At all levels, most recreational players can benefit from additional exercise to increase their strength, flexibility, and stamina.

Keep a Record

As I mentioned earlier, videoing your matches is a great way to gain insights into your team's play that you might not have remembered or been aware of yourself. Again, be sure the camera captures the entire court as you need to see how your team moves and reacts from all areas of the court.

When you sit down to watch the tape, you should both look at your strokes and movement and take note of what worked and what didn't. Pay special attention to these important areas:

- **Which team is controlling most points?** Again, the team that controls the net controls the point. Are you and your partner winning the race to the net, or are you getting caught on the defensive?
- **Are both of you mixing up your serves?** Many players fall into the pattern of serving to the same spot with the same speed and spin time after time, and then they don't understand why their opponents are ripping their returns past them.
- **Are you both being active at the net, poaching and faking?** High-level teams should try to get in at least one poach every game.
- **How was the team's movement?** Are you moving up and back as well as side to side together, or is one player breaking down and leaving holes in the court that opponents are exploiting?
- **Are you attacking your opponent's second serves and moving to the net, or are you hanging back at the baseline?** A missed first serve by your opponent is an invitation for your team to take control of the net. Hit a crosscourt return and sprint forward.
- **Is the team being patient and developing points or panicking under pressure and going for the big shot?** Trying to win points

with one shot is an impatient, low-percentage strategy. Develop your points with shot combinations and gradually break down your opponent's games and their spirit. Patience will eliminate most of your unforced errors. Remember, if you or your partner find yourselves off balance either relative to the ball (too close or far away) or the court (well behind the baseline or off to the side), lob the ball deep and give your opponent another opportunity to make an error.

If you're working with a pro, have them watch the video with you. They'll likely spot things you missed. Be honest with yourself, each other, and insist that your pro do the same.

Poaching and Faking

Poaching and faking are the ultimate intimidation tactics. When you and your partner commit to being more active at the net, your team immediately becomes stronger in two ways. First, you'll gain the ability to end points in a quick and intimidating manner. Second and, most important, you'll forever keep opposing teams off-balance.

What is Poaching?

Contrary to the opinion of many, poaching is not seeing a weak return, crossing in front of your partner, and then attacking a volley. If you're standing at the net and your opponent hits a feeble, floating return, you're supposed to go after it. That's your job!

Poaching is deciding to make a move before your opponent actually hits his shot. Keep these two thoughts in mind:

- You don't poach on a particular ball. You poach on a particular situation.
- You don't poach off your opponent's shot. You poach off your partner's shot because your partner's shot created the situation.

Here are a few mid-point poaching situations.

1. **When your opponent is hitting their inside groundstroke.** Inside means a ball toward the center of their court. When he's hitting from the center, he'll be swinging away from his body, which will likely produce a weaker shot. Plus, from the center of the court, the chances of him being able to create a sharp angle back into your alley are slim.

You can be relatively certain he'll be hitting back to your partner, so your poaching antenna should go up.

2. **When your partner is returning serve against a serve-and-volley player**. Your partner's goal is to return the serve low at his opponent's feet, forcing him to pop the ball up. Look for those low returns. When you spot one, take two quick steps forward and then, just before contact, move diagonally across the net, pick off the volley, and end the point with a strong volley of your own.

3. **When you see that your opponent is going to slice his shot.** Balls that are hit with slice move slower and tend to float.

4. **When your opponent is forced to hit a half volley or when the ball is deep and at his feet.** In both cases, his shot is likely to be slower and a bit higher.

A great way for your team to begin to incorporate poaching into your arsenal is when you're serving because you can set up the situation before the point begins. I prefer my players to do this verbally. After each point, have a brief meeting and set up the play for the next point. For example, "Serve down the middle and I'm going to go" or "Serve out wide and I'll fake." It takes two seconds, doesn't disrupt the flow of play, and both you and your partner will know what's going to happen.

Some teams like to use hand signals. However, I find that they can lead to communication breaking down several ways: the net player forgets to give the signal, the server forgets to look for the signal, or one or both players can't remember what the signals are. I prefer a brief meeting.

A Few Words of Caution

Beware of poaching when your partner hits his shot wide to the outside of the court. Wide shots are hit on an angle, and angles are often returned with angles.

Your opponent's return will often be traveling at an angle that will be too difficult for you to reach. Plus, when pulled wide, they also have a straight shot down the line so you must move to cover your alley. In this situation, it's better to fake.

How to poach

It's all about timing. If you move too soon, your opponent will see you go, have time to adapt and beat you down your alley. If you move too late, you won't be able to catch up to his ball.

As he prepares for his shot, move closer to the net. Keep your eyes glued to his racket head. When you see that he's begun his forward swing to the ball, he's committed to his shot. Take a strong split step and make your move!

Push off your outside leg and, moving diagonally toward the net, sprint across the court. By moving diagonally, you'll get closer to the net and be able to cut off your opponent's shot sooner, giving them less time to react. Think of moving toward the net strap.

Where to Hit the Volley

Since you're moving before your opponent strikes the ball, you don't know what type of shot you're going to have to play. If all goes as planned, you'll get a nice, high ball to end the point. If that happens, hit the ball hard at the feet of the opposing net player. He's closer to you and has less time to react.

If you're facing a low shot, you'll have to hit up so be sure to keep it away from the opposing net player. Volley back deep to the baseline player. Yes, your side of the court will be wide open, but your partner should be moving to cover it. You can also try a soft, crosscourt drop volley, but that's a difficult shot to execute unless you have excellent touch.

What Next

When you poach, your goal is to end the point with a strong volley. However, it doesn't always work out that way and sometimes the ball comes back. When that happens, here are your next moves:

- If you've made contact with the ball on your partner's side of the court, keep going and stay on that side. If you've struck the ball on your side, move back, and stay on your side.
- If the pace is too quick and you don't know what to do, just do something! Frequently players lose sight of where they are on the court and freeze in the middle. If this happens, just pick a side, and quickly move there. Your partner can then react accordingly.

Faking

When you fake, your goal is to distract and confuse. This can cause your opponent to change his shot mid-stroke or commit an outright error. The key is to fake early, so it looks like you've committed to poaching. Then, quickly jump back to your original position. Here are three types of fakes you can practice.

1. **The jab step.** Using your foot that's closest to the center of the court, take a very fast step toward the middle. Then, quickly return.
2. **Hop to the middle.** With this fake, you'll move both feet and hop to the center. This is a bigger, more distracting, move.
3. **Quick cross-over step.** Take a quick cross-over step and turn your entire body toward the center. Again, a more distracting move.

Two final thoughts on Poaching

1. You Must Have Thick Skin

If you're going to do your job when your partner's serving, you must be active. Whether you poach or fake, you should do some type of movement at least seventy five percent of the time. That being the case, there are going to be times when you get beaten down your alley—and that's OK. It means your opponents are aware of you. There's an old saying:

The worst doubles players never get beaten down their alley.

That's because their only net strategy is to protect their alley. As a result, they're virtually useless to the team. If your opponent is never hitting down your alley, you need to ask yourself if you're being active enough. The answer is likely no.

Always remember not to gauge your poaching success by the number of times you hit a winning volley or how often you lose the point. Until you get to a high level and develop your poaching skills, those two things may very well balance out.

A strong serving team has three advantages: effective serves that keep the receiver off-balance, aggressive players who follow their serves to the net and finally, active net players who are constantly moving, faking, and poaching.

That's three significant pressures the receiving team must deal with, and that is why, in high level doubles, service breaks are very rare.

2. Don't be This Player

The following situation frequently occurs in recreational tennis: a player at the net attempts to poach and can't reach the ball. The ball then goes past him to his partner at the baseline who subsequently misses the shot. The player who missed the shot gives his partner a nasty look, holds out his arms and says something to the effect of "You threw me off and that's why I missed the shot."

Wrong! If your partner poaches, it's your job to stay engaged and be ready to bail him out if he can't reach the ball. When that happens (if you're an active team, it will) each player should do the following:

- **If you're the player who poached and missed.** Immediately duck down so that your partner has a full view of the court.
- **If you're the baseline player.** Throw up a defensive lob. This will buy your team time to get back into a proper position. As the baseline player has the full view of the entire court (in this situation) he's the captain and should then tell his partner where to move next. For example, if the player poaching has come far over to his partner's side and slipped. The captain may tell him to stay there, feeling that he'll be able to get over to the open half of the court sooner. Or, if the poacher has just come a few feet onto his half of the court, the captain might tell him to go back. Hitting a lob gives him the time to make the decision.

Using Different Formations

Football, baseball, basketball, and soccer teams all use different formations and plays. Your team should as well. Here are two formations that your team can deploy when serving that will definitely keep your opponents off balance.

The Australian Formation

When your opponents are killing you with their crosscourt returns of serve, the Australian formation is a great tactic to throw at them.

Imagine you're serving to the ad court. Instead of standing in your normal position, move near the center mark where you would stand if you were playing singles. Your partner, Stan, who would normally be positioned in the deuce court, now stands in the ad court in front of you, diagonally facing the receiver.

By positioning Stan on the same side of the court as you, you're saying to the receiver, "You can't hit your cross-court return unless you want to hit it right to Stan, who's in a great position to hit an offensive volley." Plus, from this formation, Stan can fake or poach, the uncertainty of which will further disrupt the receiver.

Most players are grooved to return serve crosscourt most of the time. The Australian formation takes them out of their comfort zone.

The I-Formation

This is another, more advanced, formation designed to get your opponents off balance. Here, Stan lines up in the center of the court, one foot on either side of the center service line. Again, you line up as if you're playing singles.

As you prepare to serve, Stan will crouch down as low as he can. After the serve crosses the net, he'll quickly move to one side while you move to the other. This was verbally determined prior to the point. Like the Australian formation, the I-formation will keep your opponents guessing and force them to hit service returns they seldom hit.

Use these formations as often or as little as you like. Mix it up between the standard setup, the Australian, and the I-formation and remember to run your plays. Be active, fake, and poach.

If you find your team is behind, remind yourselves that momentum can change at the drop of a hat. Throwing in some different formations can definitely upset your opponent's rhythm.

Defending Against These Formations

These formations are effective because the team that's facing them often panic and have no plan. The next time you're receiving serve and the opposing team lines up in one of these formations, take a deep breath and do the following:

Australian Formation: Return the serve down the line or lob over the net player. Do not get stubborn and try to blast the ball crosscourt either through or past the net player. Against strong players, it won't work.

I-Formation: This formation is a bit trickier because you don't know which way the net player is going to move. Here's how to handle it:

- Stand a few steps farther back from your normal receiving position. This will buy you some additional time to see—and react to—your opponent's movements.
- Once you see which direction the net player is moving, you can return the ball back to the server either crosscourt or down the line.
- A return of serve down the middle of the court can also be effective because your opponents will be moving in opposite directions to cover their respective halves of the court.

When you're receiving serve, your job is to get the ball back in play. If all else fails (or even if not) a high, deep lob will always get the job done.

Be Sure Your Team is Ready

A while back, Erica, the captain of a 3.0 USTA team, asked if I'd teach her team the I-formation for their next match. When I said "No," Erica gave me a dirty look and asked why not? The conversation proceeded as follows:

Greg: Erica, when your partner is at the net, crouched down in front of you, are you confident you won't hit her in the back with your serve?
Erica: Well…not really.
Greg: Can you consistently place your serve out wide, to the center of the service box, and to the T?
Erica: Well…no.
Greg: That's why I won't teach you the I-formation.

Twelve months later, I was coaching the same team and told them that we were going to work on the I-formation. Erica immediately jumped up:

Erica: You said we shouldn't do the I-formation.
Greg: No, I said you shouldn't do the I-formation last spring. It's been a year, and everyone's worked hard to improve their serves and net skills. Now, the team **is** ready to learn the formation.

The truth is tactics and strategy are only as effective as the quality of the shots used to execute them. When Erica first asked me to teach the team the I-formation, the players' serves, movement, and volley skills were not strong enough. To use the formation would have been a disaster. A year later, everyone's skills had improved to the point where they could successfully execute the I-formation. And they did!

One Final Formation

As you move from the 3.5 to the 4.0 level and above, you'll begin to understand the great importance of controlling the net. Your opponents will as well, and your points will evolve into a race to the net. Often, you'll find yourselves with all four players up close, fighting for control of the net.

In this high-intensity situation, keep moving forward and focus on keeping your shots low, down the middle, or at your opponent's feet. Resist the urge to try a sharp angle or lob volley. In a high-level, fast paced game both are low percentages shots.

Staying on the Court

If you've made it to this final section of the book, let me first say, "thank you." I hope you'll find that the information on the previous pages helps you play better tennis.

Also, if you've read this far, you clearly have a passion for the game and want to play as much tennis as possible. The great French champion Jean Borotra once famously said:

"The only possible regret I have is the feeling that I will die without having played enough tennis."

I feel the same way. I began playing tennis over 50 years ago, still love to hit balls, and would like to play every day. Unfortunately, as the years have gone by, my body has come up with a different plan.

As I sit writing this section, I must make sure to stand up and walk around the room every few minutes. Otherwise, chronic osteoarthritis in my knees and back will begin to lock my body.

While I type and move my computer mouse along the page, I need to take a break every few hundred words to let the pain in my wrist and elbow recede. This pain is the result of hitting more than ninety-five million balls teaching tennis. That number is accurate, and if I add the countless number of balls I've struck playing the game, it's much higher.

The year I ran the New York Marathon, I was on the road training at 4:30 a.m. Then, I headed to the club and taught for eight to ten hours—one of the privileges of youth. Today, it takes about four-and-a-half hours on court before my orthopedic demons begin to stir—one of the stark realities of age.

My pain is persistent and stems from overuse, wear and tear, injuries developed over an active life. I've always believed in the "it's better to burn out than rust" approach to life so, in a weird way, I'm a little bit proud of my pain. As one world-renowned arm specialist said to me, "Greg, yours is a well-lived arm."

My situation is not unique by any means. As I write this section, twelve players at my club are unable to play due to some type of pain or injury. Injuries and the resulting pain—whether due to overuse or some type of incident—are a part of every tennis player's life, particularly as we get older.

To continue to improve and enjoy your tennis, you'll need to accept that inevitably and learn to deal with it. Specifically:

- What can you do to lessen the chance of an injury?
- How can you tell if an injury is serious?
- What can you do to overcome the injury and get back to the court as soon as possible?
- How should you deal with chronic pain?

As your game improves, the physical demands on your body increase dramatically. The constant sprinting, twisting, jumping, and stretching required to play high-level tennis place tremendous stress on every joint in your body. Here are four things that I've learned through trial and (sometimes) painful error to help you lessen your chances of getting hurt.

1. **Warm up properly.** The average recreational player's warm-up routine goes something like this:
   - Two to three minutes of uninspired, mini tennis where the players stand basically still, casually tap balls back and forth, and chat with each other.
   - A few more minutes of laidback groundstrokes, maybe a handful of volleys, and an overhead or two.

Occasionally, one or two of the players will walk to the net, place their leg over it, and then do some type of pulsating stretch which is of absolutely zero benefit. In fact, this type of stretching is more likely to hurt than warm up their body. Soon after, someone spins the racket, the player serving first says "First one in," and away they go.

This warm-up is a complete waste of time. No one has prepared their body, strokes, let alone their minds, for play. More likely, they've set themselves up to be injured. Here is a very basic routine you can do before starting to hit balls. Do this before every practice session or match. Be sure to start very slowly and do not force any of the stretches.

- **20 jumping jacks.** Stand up straight with your legs together and your arms at your sides. Bend your knees slightly, and then jump into the air. As you jump, spread your legs to be about shoulder-width apart. Stretch your arms out and over your head. Jump back to starting position. Repeat.
- **Walking knee to chest.** Start at the baseline and walk toward the net, gently pulling one knee toward your chest. Alternate legs. Go from baseline to net and back, two times.
- **Butt kicks.** Slowly jog from the baseline to the net and back, gently bringing your heels up to your butt.
- **Frankenstein walks.** Stand with your legs together and your right arm extended. Step and kick your right leg straight up. Try to touch your toe with your hand and then drop both as you walk from the baseline to the net. Repeat, twice, alternating sides.
- **Side shuffles.** Extend one leg to the side of your body and shuffle the other leg toward it. Keep your chest up and your feet straight as you continue shuffling from the baseline to the net. Go up and back twice.
- **Arm circles.** Stand with your feet shoulder-width apart and extend your arms parallel to the floor. Slowly, circle your arms forward using small and controlled motions. Gradually, make the circles bigger. Do this ten times, then reverse for ten more.
- **Forearm/wrist stretch.** Hold your right arm out in front of you, and using your left hand, gently push your hand downward. You'll feel tension in your forearm and elbow. Hold for one second and then relax and return to the starting position. Do five repetitions and repeat the stretch with your other hand.
- **Elbow stretch.** Hold your right arm in front of you with your palm up. Using your left hand, gently push your right hand down, bending at the wrists. Hold for one second. Do five repetitions and repeat the stretch with your other hand.

Note: if any of these warm-up exercise hurt in any way, don't do them!

After you play, go through a cool-down that includes static stretching. While dynamic stretches prepare your muscles for play, static stretches are slow, controlled movements that have a relaxing and lengthening effect on your muscles.

Static stretches help ease muscular stiffness and reduce the risk of muscle strains. Many trainers say that post-play stretching is more important than your pre-match routine.

Here are five static stretches you can do after playing. Hold each stretch for 20–30 seconds. Breathe comfortably, with deep breaths in through your nose, and out through your mouth.

- **Upper back stretch.** Stand tall with your feet slightly wider than shoulder-width apart and your knees slightly bent. Interlock your fingers and push your hands as far away from your chest as possible, allowing your upper back to relax. You should feel the stretch between your shoulder blades.
- **Shoulder stretch.** Stand tall, with your feet slightly wider than shoulder-width apart, and your knees slightly bent. Place your right arm, parallel with the ground across the front of your chest. Bend the left arm up and use the left forearm to ease the right arm closer to your chest. You will feel the stretch in the shoulder. Repeat with the other arm.
- **Hamstring stretch.** Sit on the ground with both legs straight out in front of you, bend the left leg, and place the sole of the left foot alongside the knee of the right leg. Allow the left leg to lie relaxed on the ground and bend forward, keeping the back straight. You will feel the stretch in the hamstring of the right leg. Repeat with the other leg.
- **Calf stretch.** Stand tall with one leg in front of the other and with your hands flat and at shoulder height against a wall. Ease your back leg farther away from the wall, keeping it straight, and press the heel firmly into the floor. Keep your hips facing the wall and your rear leg and spine in a straight line. You will feel the stretch in the calf of the rear leg. Hold the stretch and then repeat with the other leg.
- **Hip and Thigh stretch.** Stand tall with your feet approximately two shoulder widths apart. Turn your feet and face to the right. Bend your right leg so that the right thigh is parallel with the ground and the right

lower leg is vertical. Gradually lower your body, keeping your back straight, and use your arms for balance. You will feel the stretch along the front of the left thigh and along the hamstrings of the right leg. Hold a comfortable stretch and repeat by turning and facing to the left.

I know, you're very busy and don't have time to warm up before you play and certainly don't have the time to cool down after. Neither did I until I started suffering continual muscle pulls. Now, I take the time to warm up my body before my first lesson of the day-even if that lesson is at 6:30 a.m. After my on-court day is finished I make sure to do some cool down exercises so that I can be ready to go at 6:30 am tomorrow. Even if you do just a few of the warm-up and cool down exercises, you'll feel the benefit.

2. **Get stronger.** Strong muscles help protect your joints. Weight or resistance band training is great. I do both and am also a big fan of yoga. You can find plenty of exercises on the internet, but it's best to consult with a certified trainer who can design a tennis-specific program for you. He can also show you how to do the exercises properly to minimize the chance of injury. As always, consult your doctor before beginning any new activity.

3. **Stay hydrated.** Everyone tells us we should drink more water to stay hydrated. Everyone is right! Our bodies are primarily composed of water. If we deprive it of the water it needs, our muscles can tighten, cramp, and become more susceptible to injury.

How much water should we drink each day? The truth is there's no single answer. The amount of water you need will depend on many factors, such as the temperature around you and your level of activity.

For the average person, a general rule of thumb is that eight glasses of water are enough to keep you hydrated. But tennis players need more. The United States Tennis Association (USTA) recommends the following guidelines.

Before a practice session or match: Drink at least 16–20 oz. of water (one standard bottle) or electrolyte-enhanced sports drink two hours before the tennis practice or match.

During a practice session or match: Drink 4–8 oz. (4–8 normal swallows) if you're a light to medium sweater and 8–16 oz. (8–16 normal swallows) if you're a heavy sweater.

After practice or a match: Drink at least one regular-size bottle (20 oz.) of electrolyte-enhanced carbohydrate sports drink per pound of body weight lost within a two-hour period. You want to replace between 120–200 percent of the body weight lost per exercise session. If you expect to be on the court for longer than 60 minutes, the USTA recommends drinking an electrolyte-enhanced carbohydrate beverage.

4. **Eating and injuries.** Proper nutrition can't prevent you from stepping on a ball and spraining your ankle or developing tennis elbow. However, it can improve your overall health and fitness and, in the process, make injuries a little less likely.

5. **Lose those extra pounds.** When asked what most tennis players could do to improve their game, Vic Braden famously replied, "Lose ten pounds." Carrying excess weight slows you down and places additional stress on your body.

6. **If you're older, be wiser.** A few years ago, I was teaching at a corporate event where we played on hard courts. I usually play on clay and the hard courts were brutal on my body. If you're an older player or have a history of injuries, try to practice, and play on softer clay or cushioned surfaces. Both will be much easier on your joints, especially your ankles and knees.

Also, use your head. One of the best players at my club is out for the next 8-12 months because he forgot that he was 62 years old and felt it was a good idea to dive over a bench to return a wide ball. It wasn't!

7. **Get regular physicals.** Once a year, you should have a complete physical. Doing so will allow you and your doctor to develop a baseline measurement of your overall health as well as assess the risk of future health issues.

When You Do Suffer an Injury

When you do suffer some type of injury, the first step is to assess its severity.

Use these categories:

1. **Level 1:** These injuries could be minor aches and pains, causing soreness in your back, shoulder, arm, or legs. These areas may loosen up as you play or may require a few days off.
2. **Level 2:** Any pain that stays with you for more than three days is a level 2 injury. If you see swelling, or the pain persists for more than three days, then the injury is more significant. Examples of a level 2 injury include a sprained ankle, strained back, or persistent pain. Monitor the injury and remember the time-tested acronym, RICE:

Rest, Ice, Compress (with an Ace bandage), and **Elevate** the injury.

You can also try some over the counter, anti-inflammatory medicines. Do not try to play through a level 2 injury. If you don't notice significant improvement within 36 hours, definitely see your doctor.

Level 3: Level 3 injuries are more serious and will force you off the courts for an extended period. These injuries, such as tennis elbow, may require physical therapy, and in cases like a torn meniscus, surgery.

Chronic Pain

During my years on the court, I've suffered every level of injury mentioned above. I've had three knee surgeries and too many strains and sprains to count. As a result, I deal with pain daily. It's a hazard of my profession that I'm willing to accept because I love what I do.

My doctor once asked me what my fitness goals were. It really made me pause and take stock. At this point in my life, my primary fitness goal—outside of maintaining my overall health—is to be teaching on the tennis court, for as long as I possibly can. I still love to play, but if I play too often or too hard, I pay the price over the next few days. As a result, I play much less than I used to.

I love to work out and work out hard. However, with my fitness goal always in the front of my mind, my workouts have changed dramatically as I've gotten older. Running and lifting heavy weights have been replaced by resistance bands, the Peloton, and Bikram Yoga. These provide me with the cardio, strength, and flexibility workouts I crave, yet they don't pound on my joints and leave me in pain the next day on the court.

I have an icing routine for my arm, knees, and back that takes about forty minutes every day. I also get regular massages. These help me to keep my body functioning and relatively limber.

If your goal is to play tennis for the rest of your life, you must take your health seriously. If you feel pain or suffer an injury, follow the advice above and always err on the side of caution.

Don't be stubborn and try to play through the pain. This usually does far more harm than good and could turn a minor injury into a major one. If your pain doesn't ease in a few days, see your doctor!

Again, thank you for taking the time to read my book. If you have any questions or would like to contact me, please feel free to do so at GMoran@4seasonstennis.com.

Play often, work hard, and above all, have fun!